Automated Metadata in Multimedia Information Systems: Creation, Refinement, Use in Surrogates, and Evaluation

Synthesis Lectures on Information Concepts, Retrieval, and Services

Editor
Gary Marchionini, *University of North Carolina, Chapel Hill*

© Springer Nature Switzerland AG 2022
Reprint of original edition © Morgan & Claypool 2009

Automated Metadata in Multimedia Information Systems: Creation, Refinement, Use in Surrogates, and Evaluation
Michael G. Christel

ISBN: 978-3-031-01130-6   paperback

ISBN: 978-3-031-02258-6   ebook

DOI: 10.1007/978-3-031-02258-6

A Publication in the Springer series

SYNTHESIS LECTURES ON INFORMATION CONCEPTS, RETRIEVAL, AND SERVICES # 2

Lecture #2

Series Editor: Gary Marchionini, University of North Carolina, Chapel Hill

Series ISSN Pending

Automated Metadata in Multimedia Information Systems: Creation, Refinement, Use in Surrogates, and Evaluation

Michael G. Christel
Carnegie Mellon University

SYNTHESIS LECTURES ON INFORMATION CONCEPTS, RETRIEVAL, AND SERVICES # 2

ABSTRACT

Improvements in network bandwidth along with dramatic drops in digital storage and processing costs have resulted in the explosive growth of multimedia (combinations of text, image, audio, and video) resources on the Internet and in digital repositories. A suite of computer technologies delivering speech, image, and natural language understanding can automatically derive descriptive metadata for such resources. Difficulties for end users ensue, however, with the tremendous volume and varying quality of automated metadata for multimedia information systems. This lecture surveys automatic metadata creation methods for dealing with multimedia information resources, using broadcast news, documentaries, and oral histories as examples. Strategies for improving the utility of such metadata are discussed, including computationally intensive approaches, leveraging multimodal redundancy, folding in context, and leaving precision-recall tradeoffs under user control. Interfaces building from automatically generated metadata are presented, illustrating the use of video surrogates in multimedia information systems. Traditional information retrieval evaluation is discussed through the annual National Institute of Standards and Technology TRECVID forum, with experiments on exploratory search extending the discussion beyond fact-finding to broader, longer term search activities of learning, analysis, synthesis, and discovery.

KEYWORDS

multimedia, digital video library, automated metadata generation, speech recognition, image processing, named entity extraction, video surrogate, information retrieval, evaluation, TRECVID

Preface

The author has had the privilege of working with the Informedia digital video understanding research group at Carnegie Mellon University since its beginnings in 1994. He has witnessed first-hand the benefits and shortcomings of speech recognition, image processing, and natural language technologies for automatically generating descriptions for multimedia repositories. This lecture reports on those experiences through the years, drawing heavily from Informedia examples and studies. Each chapter concludes with a set of reflective exercises branching out from this Informedia work. These exercises can be used as supplemental assignments by teachers or as suggestions for further exploration by interested readers.

Table of Contents

C H A P T E R   1

Evolution of Multimedia Information Systems: 1990–2008

This lecture discusses the role of automatically produced descriptors for multimedia source material, based on more than 14 years of work by the author with the Informedia research group at Carnegie Mellon University (www.informedia.cs.cmu.edu). This opening section defines terms in setting the scope for the lecture.

What is multimedia? The word is derived from "multiple media" with the Merriam-Webster Online Dictionary definition staying true to that derivation: "using, involving, or encompassing several media." However, debates have raged for years in venues such as the annual ACM Multimedia Conference as to what constitutes "multimedia" work and hence what is in scope for the multimedia venue. Is a newspaper photograph with a text caption multimedia? The picture is a visual image, but the caption can be considered a different media element, a textual one. Indeed, the Merriam-Webster Online Dictionary definition for multimedia as a noun lists text as a media form: "multimedia (noun): a technique (as the combining of sound, video, and text) for expressing ideas (as in communicaton, entertainment, or art) in which several media are employed." This latter definition widens the expressive scope considerably, too broad for a single lecture. By discussing "multimedia information systems," this lecture will center on multimedia for communicaton, rather than for entertainment or art.

In addition, this lecture will sidestep the issue of whether captioned still images such as newspaper photos constitute multimedia. For a newspaper photo, both the picture and the text are discrete, with no temporal dimension. In constrast, audio and video are continuous media types with a temporal flow; the information at time point $N+1$ building on what was presented at time N. Although a generous definition of multimedia allows for the combination of at least two elements from continuous *and discrete* media types, in this lecture the scope is further narrowed to require at least one continuous media type. The temporal dimension is a key component of the automated processing and summarization techniques discussed in later sections. The temporal dimension is also a huge motivation for pursuing automated metadata generation. Even with a relatively small set of 1000 hours of video, it is costly and tedious to watch that 1000 hours and annotate by hand its contents, costing 4000 hours of labor at the conservative ratio of 4:1 for such a tagging effort. For a user interested in a 5-minute section, it is frustrating and inefficient to wade through hours of material in the 1000-hour set. Requiring continuous media in this discussion of multimedia information systems permits an emphasis on dealing with temporal redundancy.

Finally, it is now presumed that when one talks of multimedia information systems, one implies that all media types are digitized, that each type—whether audio, video, or text—is accessible as computer data. When the author first began work with computer-controlled video in the 1980s, this was not the case. A typical computer-presented video system had an analog videodisc player hooked up to the computer through a serial port and the computer merely passed on instructions to the videodisc player to play, pause, and seek, with no chance to process the bits of video information: that video information was in analog form, not digital. With the advent of Digital Video Interactive (DVI) technology from RCA in the late 1980s and then the explosive growth of computational power and storage capacity, digital video was born and blossomed, to the point now that analog video information systems based on videodiscs, magnetic tapes, or other storage media are considered obsolete. The task of finding a 5-minute video clip of interest from a thousand hour-long videotapes can be incredibly frustrating, based on conversations with archivists and library researchers. Digitizing video opens it up for numerous automated metadata generation techniques and indexing strategies for nonlinear retrieval, which can promote better understanding in users and more efficient navigation and exploration.

Digital data are proliferating exponentially, as witnessed by the accumulating amount of content on the World Wide Web. In the 1990s, web video data were comparatively sparse, but during the past decade there has been an explosive growth in web video content as well. Various video players today allow video retrieval by vast numbers of Web users, with major ones including Adobe's Flash, Apple's QuickTime, Microsoft's Windows Media Player, and RealNetworks' RealPlayer. However, video is a difficult media type to access efficiently, requiring significant amounts of viewing time to play through linearly, comparatively large storage requirements to buffer and keep locally, and tremendous patience to download when network congestion or legacy hardware limits one's download bandwidth. In light of this situation, many multimedia interface researchers have focused on developing alternate representations for video, enabling users to quickly assess whether a video clip is worthy of further inspection and providing quick navigation within the clip itself. These representations have been called multimedia abstractions [1], video abstracts [2], and surrogates [3]. This lecture will discuss these representations and the techniques producing metadata that drive them.

The world of multimedia has changed radically in the past 20 years. In the early 1990s, the huge cost of video and varying encoding standards were problematic. Multimedia information typically was stored in libraries as analog tape, accessed through text index cards and descriptions. The shift of materials from analog to digital storage was hampered by cost but also the variability among numerous digital video compression standards coming from various international commercial and academic institutions. The Moving Picture Experts Group (MPEG) defined the MPEG-1 and MPEG-2 standards to address the need for standardization. The MPEG group was founded in 1988 with the mandate of developing standards for coded representation of moving pictures, audio, and their combination.

Analog video has tremendous amounts of data within it: at National Television Standards Committee transmission, the frame rate is 29.97 frames per second, with each frame at 640 × 480 resolution. Each frame represented as an uncompressed digital image requires more than 1 MB of space, so an hour of uncompressed video consumes more than 100 GB of storage. Hence, holding a thousand hours was impractical in that 1990 timeframe. Compression was necessary to reduce the storage and transmission costs for digital video. MPEG-1 was designed to get Video Home System (VHS)-quality video (352 × 240 resolution, 30 frames per second) to a fixed data rate of 1.5 Mbits/second so that it could play from a regular compact disc. MPEG-2 was designed for coding video at higher data rates and in an interlaced format, suitable for professional broadcast video and enabling the launch of the DVD market. Although MPEG-1 is lossy (some information is lost from the original analog video form and compression artifacts may be visually noticeable), it allowed a thousand hours of video to be stored in a terabyte of space, at a VHS quality accepted by consumers. The 1.5 Mbits/second transfer rate allowed the video to be broadcast and played through a network of computers. These criteria allowed the Informedia research project to be launched in 1994.

The terabyte of storage for 1000 hours of video for an early 1990s Informedia video library cost $1 million, with that terabyte now approaching $100. The 4 orders-of-magnitude savings enabled the explosive growth of video on the Internet, as evidenced by user-generated video hosting sites such as YouTube. In November 2007, more than 75% of U.S. Internet users watched a streaming or progressive video download. Americans viewed nearly 9.5 billion online videos that month, 2.9 billion of which occurred at YouTube [4]. The adoption of digital video standards, dramatic reduction in storage costs, and growth in network capacity from 1990 until today allow multimedia information systems to be processed, indexed, and shared in new ways beyond text-only representations.

1.1   INTRODUCTION TO THE INFORMEDIA PROJECT

The Informedia Project at Carnegie Mellon University began in 1994 with funding from the National Science Foundation, Defense Advanced Research Projects Agency, and National Aeronautics and Space Administration, at a time when digital video was still relatively new. The management of a terabyte of information, a thousand hours of MPEG-1 format video, required more than simply making the video accessible to computer algorithms, i.e., simply digitizing the video did not make the task easier of finding 5 minutes of relevant material from a thousand hours. Rather, through segmenting, describing, and indexing the multimedia information, the terabyte of data becomes more manageable and accessible. Informedia research applied speech recognition, image processing, and natural language processing to digital video so that it could be:

- Deconstructed into segments and shots, with each story segment consisting of a continuous range of video and/or audio deemed conceptually similar, and a shot being "contiguous frames representing a continuous action in time or space" [5];
- Analyzed to derive additional descriptors, i.e., metadata, for creating alternate representations of the video;
- Augmented with indices of the metadata associated with segments to allow for the fast searching and retrieval of segments and shots.

Since the start of Informedia project, three major thrusts have occurred in the multimedia information retrieval (IR) research community that have shaped the sequence of project work, and are reflected in the rest of this lecture's discussion. The thrusts are a concern for openly accessible community benchmarks for evaluation, addressing user information needs through high-level visual concepts, and supporting collection understanding and information exploration beyond just a ranked set of results for a particular query.

First, as researchers across the globe began investigating multimedia IR and, in particular, video IR, there was a concern that without benchmarks, it would be difficult to establish the current state of the field, be able to replicate results, and chart scientific progress. The National Institute of Standards and Technology Text Retrieval Conference (TREC) Video Retrieval Evaluation forum (TRECVID), began in 2001 as an international benchmarking forum devoted to research in automatic segmentation, indexing, and content-based retrieval of digital video. TRECVID experiments form the framework for many shot-based retrieval experiments cited later in this lecture.

Second, can high level concepts bridge the semantic gap? In searching through multimedia archives, digital imagery indexing based on low-level image features such as color and texture, or manually entered text annotations, often fail to meet the user's information needs, i.e., there is often a semantic gap produced by "the lack of coincidence between the information that one can extract from the visual data and the interpretation that the same data have for a user in a given situation" [6]. Low-level features such as histograms in the HSV, RGB, and YUV color space, Gabor texture or wavelets, and structure through edge direction histograms and edge maps can be accurately and automatically extracted from imagery, but studies have repeatedly confirmed the difficulty of addressing information needs with such low-level features [7, 8]. Other TRECVID-based studies have established the benefits of queries against high-level semantic concepts such as outdoor, road, and building for broadcast news shot retrieval [9, 10]. This lecture discusses the derivation and use of high-level semantic concepts to assist in multimedia retrieval and its promise to bridge the semantic gap by providing more accessible visual content descriptors. Hurdles include what concepts to supply, the level of accuracy in automatic detection of such concepts, the applicability of concepts to user information needs, and whether users can correctly choose what concepts to apply in the face of certain needs.

Finally, as soon as the Informedia video corpus grew from tens to hundreds of hours, the interface and processing techniques focusing on the individual video segment proved insufficient: users were overwhelmed with information returned from text or image queries and had no easy way to understand returned collections of video. Information visualization addresses such collection-level understanding. Informedia work progressed toward developing and testing browsing interfaces for appreciating and navigating collections rather than sequentially looking through a ranked list of segments. Work on exploratory interfaces built from automated metadata closes out the lecture, with reflections on the difficulties in evaluating multimedia information exploration.

1.2   REFLECTIONS/EXERCISES

As mentioned in the Preface, each section of the lecture concludes with a set of reflective exercises branching out from the reported Informedia work. These exercises can be used as supplemental assignments by teachers or as suggestions for further exploration by interested readers. This first set of exercises covers both the introductory definitions of terms such as "multimedia" and the evolution of multimedia system capabilities.

1. Ramesh Jain was the first editor-in-chief of *IEEE Multimedia* for several years and remains very active as a multimedia researcher. He helped to formulate the definition of multimedia appearing in the work of Rowe and Jain [11], and wrote several columns in *IEEE Multimedia* and devoted many blog posts to the changing definition through the years. Investigate Jain's definitions from sources at different times, and consider whether captioned newspaper photos, music libraries, Flickr, and YouTube would be considered multimedia information systems by his definitions.

2. Suppose you had a multimedia library of all the blockbuster Hollywood movies. Consider whether the following tasks would be easy or difficult in both 1990 and today: (a) find all instances of Harrison Ford; (b) find all instances of Harrison Ford as Indiana Jones; (c) find Indiana Jones saying he hates snakes; (d) find him in a close-up looking at dangerous animal or object; (e) find him looking sensitive.

3. Consider different genres of video: broadcast news, sports, commercial films, consumer home video. All video can be decomposed into frames. Contrast the ease of segmenting

such video into a hierarchy of frames, shots, "scenes," and story segments. Provide a definition of what you consider a shot boundary (the break between different shots), a scene boundary, and a story boundary. What is your definition of scene? Consider the comments made by these authors in designing browsing interfaces for different genres of video [12].

· · · ·

CHAPTER 2

Survey of Automatic Metadata Creation Methods

As defined in the Merriam Webster Online Dictionary, metadata is "data that provides information about other data." An overview of metadata for imagery discusses the broad range of metadata possibilities [13]. It can be free-form text or in structured form making use of controlled vocabularies. Metadata can describe the multimedia resource as a whole, or can describe a portion of it, e.g., a particular frame from within a video sequence. Metadata can serve a variety of purposes [13]:

> [Metadata] might be used to help us to find the resource (resource discovery metadata), or might tell us what it is (descriptive metadata). It might tell us where the resource has come from, who owns it and how it can be used (provenance and rights metadata). It might describe how the digital resource was created (technical metadata), how it is managed (administrative metadata), and how it can be kept into the future (preservation metadata). Or it might, as mentioned earlier, help us to relate this digital resource with other resources (structural metadata).

This lecture focuses on automatic indexing, which applies best toward descriptive metadata and resource discovery metadata where the resource may be a small snippet within a larger multimedia object, e.g., finding the relevant minute from a set of hour-long broadcasts. Describing a video at various levels of granularity by manual effort is costly, error-prone, and incomplete, leading to a growing number of international researchers investigating the problem of automatically generating descriptors for video, as evidenced by the increased participation in Text Retrieval Conference (TREC) Video Retrieval Evaluation (TRECVID) through the years.

To illustrate the need for automatic indexing, let us look at an example where a wealth of detailed information is available: Hollywood movies. If we consider a movie such as the classic *Citizen Kane*, we might have a title, author, director, actors, an abstract summarizing the movie, and a movie script listing and describing each scene, a portion of which is shown in Figure 2.1.

Even this comprehensive script clearly leaves out a large amount of detail that is visible in the scene. There are just too many visual details to describe, at different levels of specificity, even

```
        DISSOLVE: INT. KANE'S BEDROOM -

        FAINT DAWN - 1940

    A very long shot of Kane's enormous bed,

    silhouetted against the enormous window.
```

FIGURE 2.1: Snippet of detail from the script of *Citizen Kane*.

with a budget that supports manual authoring of text descriptions. Information within the video can range from specific details to instances of objects to abstract emotional conveyance, reflecting the Panofsky–Shatford mode/facet matrix of specific, generic, and abstract subjects of pictures [14]. Interpretations of what the video is about can be colored by personal experience and culture. Reasoning about imagery is complex [15], with words alone as shown in Figure 2.1 unlikely to capture all the connotations that a viewer might perceive.

The art historian Panofsky, working with Renaissance images, defined three levels of semantic significance in imagery: preiconographic, iconographic, and iconologic [16, 17] . The preiconographic index includes descriptions of the work's pure form, e.g., blue or red, bed, and window. The iconographic index leverages from social and cultural knowledge to identify specifics, e.g., "Kane's bedroom" or perhaps even "1940" or "dawn." The iconologic index includes symbolic meaning of an image such as "peaceful." Information scientist Sara Shatford applied Panofsky's model to indexing images, relabeling his terms as generic, specific, and abstract, and breaking each of these levels into four facets: who, what, where, and when [14]. The descriptor argued over by art historians and viewers—"why" an image is as it is and what abstract iconologic intrinsic meaning does it convey—will not be emphasized in this lecture. Both manual and automated indexing measures have a better chance of success with producing *generic* and *specific* descriptors for still and moving imagery, as these are more objective descriptors than addressing *abstract* layers [18].

Jaimes and colleagues published a pyramid conceptual framework for classifying visual content attributes [19, 20], which incorporates the Panofsky–Shatford model within its 10 levels. The four topmost levels of the pyramid describe images with syntax/perceptual information, wereas the six bottom levels describe generic object or scene, specific object or scene, and abstract object or scene. A review of the field from Jaimes et al. [19] presents the following overview and references across the 10 levels with respect to automated processing, from the topmost syntactic level down to the abstract semantic level requiring the most knowledge.

Type/techique: The most basic general visual characteristics of the image or video sequence, e.g., image categories such as color or black and white, X-ray, photograph, watercolor, or oil medium [21].

Global distribution: Classifying images or video sequences based on their global content in terms of low-level perceptual features such as spectral sensitivity (color), and frequency sensitivity (texture); global color histogram or global texture has been used in support of query by example searches [21, 22]. Results for users are often unsatisfying, e.g., Figure 2.2 shows a search with an image of a rain forest returning images of many different objects, semantically very different but sharing the same global color blue-green concentration.

Local structure: Concerned with the extraction and characterization of components, from lowest level dot, line, tone, and texture to dividing the visual into an $M \times N$ grid and having color and texture attributes for each spatial grid box, to local shape and two-dimensioanal geometry. Local structure provides query by user sketch functionality as first exemplified in Query By Image Content (QBIC) [22].

Global composition: The arrangement of basic elements given by the local structure, the spatial layout of elements in the image addressing concepts such as balance, symmetry, center of attention, and viewing angle. Global templates based on low-level features can be learned by the system [23], with query-by-shape functionality that supports retrieval of similarly shaped images as shown in Figure 2.3. Here, the query is a rounded head and shoulders shape in front of straight line image elements.

These four levels introduced by Jaimes and colleagues discuss the syntax/perceptual information in imagery, requiring no world knowledge to perform indexing, so automatic techniques can be used to extract relevant information on these levels. However, having only metadata from these levels produces the semantic gap discussed earlier: computers are excellent with such syntactic extraction and indexing, but humans mainly use higher-level attributes to describe, classify, and search. Systems such as QBIC failed to achieve broad appeal and commercial success because human searchers wanted more than query by color, shape, texture, and sketching capabilities, rather looking toward

FIGURE 2.2: Example of syntactically correct matches of blue-green images to blue-green key, but with results spanning a variety of objects unlikely to be the true information targets for a user.

FIGURE 2.3: Example of syntactically correct shape matches of news anchor person to other news anchor people.

semantics as overviewed in the remaining six levels of the Jaimes pyramid and addressing the Pan-ofksy–Shatford mode/facet matrix of specific, generic, and abstract subjects of imagery.

Generic objects: Generic objects are basic level categories such as car or building. A great deal of work in object recognition allows indexing of generic objects in constrained domains [24]. More recent techniques, however, have focused on generic objects in less constrained domains. Examples include naked people and horses [25] and faces [26].

Generic scene: Generic scene classification labels visual material as a whole based on the set of all of the objects it contains and their arrangement; examples include labeling as indoor or outdoor [27], city or landscape [28], and different types of nature photographs [29].

Specific objects: A named instance of a generic object, e.g., the Empire State Building. Automatically mapping objects detected in images or video to their specific names brings in the need for additional modalities such as captions or audio to provide specifics in nonvisual information as labels for visual information [30, 31].

Specific scene: A named instance of a generic scene, e.g., Manhattan by Central Park. Carnegie Mellon University (CMU) Informedia researchers have used multiple modalities to automatically tag scenes with specifics, i.e., using a learning-based approach to annotate shots of news video with locations extracted from the video transcript, based on features from multiple video modalities including syntactic structure of transcript sentences, speaker identity, and temporal video structure [32].

Abstract objects: Specialized or interpretive knowledge of what objects in the image represent, highly subjective.

Abstract scene: What the image as a whole represents, also highly subjective.

The remainder of this section presents automatic techniques to derive such visual descriptors drawn primarily from Informedia work as that will be later illustrated in the interface examples. Aural and text processing is introduced as well, as a necessary means to leverage additional modalities to more accurately classify video and imagery as specific scenes or objects. The abstract levels, abstract objects, and scenes, will not be addressed further, and these have remained outside the scope of annual TRECVID benchmarking information retrieval tasks as well. TRECVID has emphasized the middle layers, particularly generic and specific objects and events [33].

2.1   AURAL PROCESSING

For many genres of video, such as broadcast news, lectures, and documentaries, the spoken narrative provides descriptive detail pertaining to the audiovisual contents. The narrative allows for success in news shot retrieval [34] and enables automated metadata extraction supporting specific scene and specific object descriptions. Perhaps the most common question asked to the CMU Informedia group has been the quality of automatic speech-recognized text, making it an early focus area for the research.

Automatic speech recognition (ASR) processes spoken audio and produces a text transcript, with CMU Sphinx being one of the most popular university-based ASR systems in the early 1990s and leading to commercial efforts at Apple, Microsoft, and elsewhere. The quality of ASR output depends greatly on the input audio signal and how well the speaker matches the training data that was used for the ASR system, with some factors shown in Figure 2.4. Historically, most ASR systems were trained with North American English-speaking male adult speakers using a *Wall Street Journal* corpus of material.

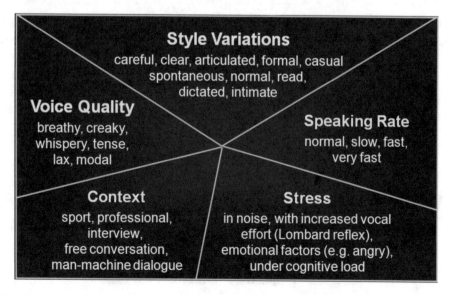

FIGURE 2.4: Factors affecting automatic speech recognition quality.

The knowledge sources used in ASR include acoustic modeling (e.g., the specific phonemes in North American English speech), the lexicon, and the language model, as shown in Figure 2.5. Low-quality ASR output can sometimes be addressed by improving one or more of these sources. For example, lectures on computer science will use words and phrases such as "algorithm" and "data abstraction" much more than a default *Wall Street Journal*-based language model, and so a specific language model tuned to computer science dialog would better suit ASR of computer science lectures. Without such tuning, if the default language model has high occurrence of a term such as "criminal infraction" and none for "data abstraction" then speech with the latter may get incorrectly transcribed as the former. Similarly, the lexicon can bring in terms such as "Turing" that are in a computer science corpus but not in the default training corpus that historically has tens of thousands of words but still omits proper names and specialized terms that hold value in a given domain. More details on ASR specifics are provided in a separate lecture devoted to the topic [35].

Speech recognition is an imperfect technology, and—depending on the audio quality of the input video and the amount of processing time devoted to the task—the resulting transcript will have a medium to high word error rate. Word error rate is the typical metric used to gauge ASR accuracy, and is defined as the sum of word insertion, deletion, and substitution errors. Figure 2.6 shows the word error rate ranges for different types of video with the CMU Sphinx 3 recognizer in the late 1990s.

By far the most problematic video that Informedia attempted to process with ASR has been advertisements in television broadcasts. The main problem with such audio is that the music interferes with the spoken narrative, and the narrative itself may be edited with compressed silences to squeeze into 30-second commercial spots. The result is quite poor performance, as seen in Figure 2.6. When the audio is captured cleanly, using a close-talking microphone in a quiet environment

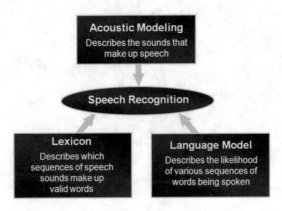

FIGURE 2.5: Knowledge sources for speech recognition.

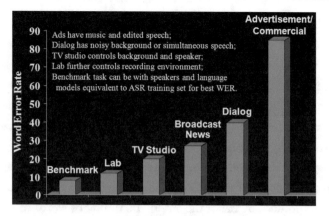

FIGURE 2.6: ASR word error rate in tests of different data sets.

with a speaker sharing common attributes with the acoustic model (e.g., native American English speaker), lexicon (e.g., saying only words known to the speech recognizer), and language model (e.g., saying statements represented with same frequency in the recognizer), then results are quite good. In initial Informedia experiments on American broadcast news data in 1994, the word error rate was 65% using the Sphinx 2 recognizer. In later tests with the current Sphinx 3 speech recognizer trained on 66 hours of news broadcasts, the error rate on broadcast news stories was about 24%. This word error rate was further reduced to about 19% through the use of general news language models interpolated with "news of the day" currency, as obtained from the web sites of CNN, Reuters, and the AP newswire services. Additional improvements potentially can be made by automatically training the recognizer with volumes of broadcast television speech coupled with their closed-captioned transcripts [36].

Despite the relatively high word error rates, early Informedia experiments suggested that the information retrieval effectiveness can be adequate despite the transcription mistakes by the speech recognition module [37, 38]. Other experiments showed that effects of words missing in the recognizer's lexicon could be mitigated [39, 40]. Specifically, word error rates up to 25% did not significantly impact information retrieval and error rates of 50% still provided 85–95% of the recall and precision relative to fully accurate transcripts in the same retrieval system [37]. From these IR experiments, we learned that even relatively high word error rates in the speech recognition nevertheless permit relatively effective information retrieval, which was investigated more openly and completely in the TREC Spoken Document Retrieval (SDR) track from 1997 to 2000. The track ended in 2000 with the conclusion that retrieval of excerpts from broadcast news using ASR for transcription permits relatively effective information retrieval, even with word error rates of 30% [41, 42].

Research and development continues with ASR, with the Sphinx 4 speech recognition system slated for delivery in 2008. ASR-specific research topics and details are overviewed on the Sphinx 4 wiki web site [43], as well as in the separate lecture devoted to ASR [35]. Regardless of which ASR engine is used for multimedia information processing, the lessons outlined here from Informedia work still hold relevance. That is, despite the errors in ASR from speech variations (Figure 2.4) or out-of-date or too small knowledge sources (Figure 2.5), ASR-produced text still succeeds in supporting content-based indexing of specifics in video, at least for the news video genre benchmarked in TREC SDR. In cases where transcripts are supplied through human labor, as with closed-captioning or a fully transcribed oral history corpus such as The HistoryMakers, ASR engines can still provide metadata too tedious to produce by hand: the automatic timing of words to when they are spoken. The automatic alignment of speech to text enables a rich set of interfaces and supports efficient navigation to the temporal neighborhood of interest within a video.

Other aural automated detectors delivering high accuracy include silence detection and speaker change, both which can be used as input data for locating story change points, i.e., boundaries at which to divide a long broadcast into story segments. Speaker identification, i.e., labeling the speaker with the same label if he or she is a repeat speaker, is a feature of the commercial SAIL ASR engine [44], which has been used with much success in current Informedia work with news video, documentaries, and oral history interviews. As with ASR and Figure 2.6, the accuracy of speaker identification depends considerably on the quality of the input signal.

In addition to transcript generation and alignment, aural processing can categorize the audio as music or speech, and detect aural events such as crowd cheers, laughter, gunshots, and explosions. The automatic detection of applause and cheering with sports footage has been used to automatically highlight scoring events [45, 46], leading to patented applications within Mitsubishi digital video recorders, for example, to extract sports highlights [47]. A survey of how audio events can be incorporated into video content indexing is given by Xiong and colleagues [48]. Cai et al. [49] argue that unsupervised content discovery, without the need for training data, will better generalize to a broad set of audio streams. They use low-level aural features and spectral clustering to place sounds in categories such as speech, music, noise, and applause [49]. Such additional aural processing provides labels for multimedia sequences that can be used to support faceted search (e.g., just video with music), or derive higher-order classification that folds in visual attributes as well (e.g., humor/comedy classification based on laughter and face close-ups). As soon as the audio event migrates from lower level syntactical types such as silence vs. nonsilence, automated classification accuracy drops, but accuracy is regained by limiting the input genre. For example, a gunshot detector works well in surveillance video where the only loud noise would be a gunshot, but would trigger many false alarms if run on sports video where the crack of a baseball bat would get mislabeled as a gunshot. Similarly, the patented Mitsubishi sports scoring detector working from crowd noise works well against soccer video, where scores are accompanied by a high aural volume of cheers, but works poorly for basketball video, where scores are distributed throughout the game. By limiting the input genre, sounds can be more accurately classified into higher-order audio events such as gunshots, cheers, excited speech, and sports highlights.

2.2   VISUAL PROCESSING

Online visual information has proliferated in the past few years, ranging from ever-growing personal digital photo collections to professional news and documentary video libraries. Services such as Google Image Search provide a means for looking up Web-based images, mostly by using the text associated with the image rather than visual processing of the image itself. The ASR techniques discussed in the previous section can be used to supply spoken narrative text for video, with some archives already having the text metadata in hand for closed-caption services for the hearing impaired. Video search services can provide access to digital imagery through such associated text, an approach called concept-based visual indexing [50, 51] where linguistic cues are used to represent, index, and retrieve nonlinguistic visual imagery.

This section considers the challenge of multimedia information retrieval in the absence of such text: Does automated visual processing have something to offer? In many situations, text accompanying visuals may be unavailable, irrecoverable, or inapplicable. People are reluctant to annotate their photo collections, unwilling to invest the time to label images with text descriptors, even when the annotation can be done through a speech interface, so images may never receive the benefit of text keyword associations [52]. Some video collections such as silent films, home video, or stock footage without narrative may not have transcripts. International broadcasts often lack closed-caption texts, and if present the multitude of languages introduces the complexity of cross-lingual retrieval, so the narrative may not be easily recoverable. Text annotations for images will likely be incomplete, because different people have been shown to label the same images with different words [50], and the text may not document the aspect of the image of interest to the user performing the search [6]. Even if a transcript is available for a source such as broadcast news, the information need may be highly visual, with the desired material shown in the news video but never mentioned in the transcript.

With content-based information retrieval (CBIR), images and video can be indexed by pixel-level image attributes such as color, texture, edges, or shape, or classified with higher-level semantic features such as people or settings. Yang et al. [53] compare the *concept*-based and *content*-based approaches: concept-based visual indexing has high expressive power that can easily communicate with users but still involves information loss in transforming visual materials into text, and requires more intensive human labor. In contrast, CBIR methods can be automated, and so have the potential to be more economical as well as address the users' visual needs. Through content-based indexing, the image is analyzed and compared to other images according to similarities in low-level image feature representations [6, 55]. CBIR is valuable for certain tasks, such as face retrieval and fingerprints, and is powerful for queries focusing on texture, color, or overall image similarity, but it may lead to a visually similar but conceptually disjoint match (as shown in Figure 2.2). The video analysis community has long struggled to bridge the gap from successful, low-level syntactic feature analysis (color histograms, texture, shape) to semantic content description of video. Although rich feature spaces can be developed to create a correspondence between lower level features and human perception, the resulting high-dimensional space is then not well suited for fast, interactive access through indexing [55]. Technology-driven visual content indexing approaches have been published with great success rates but merited little or no use in fielded systems, in part because of the often-mentioned "semantic gap" in the multimedia research community, i.e., the lack of coincidence between the information that one can automatically extract from the visual data and the interpretation that the same data has for a user in a given situation [6]. Systems such as QBIC retrieve images based on attributes such as color or texture [22], but studies have questioned the utility of image searching according to such low-level properties [7] and QBIC never achieved commercial success. The semantic gap makes it difficult for the user to formulate queries against the image library [56].

One plausible solution is to use a set of intermediate (textual) descriptors, rooted in an ontology, that can be reliably applied to visual scenes. Many researchers have been developing automatic feature classifiers such as face, people, sky, grass, plane, outdoors, soccer goals, or buildings [57], showing that perhaps these classifiers will reach the level of maturity needed for their use as effective filters for video retrieval. It is an ongoing research issue as to how to best represent the high level semantics of a video shot, given the current techniques for automatic lower-level feature extraction [34]. A concern is that automated classifiers for such higher-level features are considerably less accurate than those that detect color, shape, or texture low-level features. An open question is the effect of feature availability, applicability, and accuracy of automated feature classification on multimedia retrieval [53]. The National Institute of Standards and Technology-sponsored TRECVID community annually challenges international researchers to demonstrate the effectiveness of *content*-based indexing—specifically, the contribution of the visual information channel—for searches against video collections [33, 58]. In recent years, the multimedia research community has invested in developing a Large-Scale Concept Ontology for Multimedia (LSCOM), whereby semantic features such as "road" or "people" can be used for video retrieval [59]. LSCOM work looks to assemble on the order of a thousand automatically detectable semantic visual features, building from earlier TRECVID evaluations, MediaMill work with 101 visual features [60], and Columbia University work with 374 features [61]. TRECVID evaluation on automatic feature detection and search tasks allows the evolution of these feature classifiers to be tracked to see if they increase in accuracy and utility over time, with utility to be addressed in Chapter 5. The overall accuracy of most automatic visual feature classifiers is still quite poor, e.g., the mean average precision (MAP) of the Columbia 374 models was less than 0.1. By comparison, the MAP of the best Web text search engines has been reported at 0.65 [62], as discussed by Hauptmann et al. [63]. Feature detector accuracies vary widely according to feature, as seen in the annual TRECVID reports, with some such as sports scoring well and others such as police and animal scoring near zero. Overall, the accuracies are so low that one might conclude there is no utility left for such automated visual processing, except for three insights. First, sometimes classification accuracy can be high for particular features, as with text and face detection to be discussed further later. Second, as with aural event processing, by limiting the input genre substantially higher success can be obtained. For example, a soccer goal net detector would trigger many false positives in city scenes with vertical line edges and netlike patterns, but if given only soccer video it can succeed by differentiating the common green field backdrop from the white colors and edges seen with the net. Limiting the genre to a particular sport has resulted in numerous multimedia information retrieval publications of visual feature success over the years, with the feature tied to a particular sport as well. See also a lecture devoted to the topic of human activity detection within primarily surveillance style video [64]. Third, the simulated experiments of Hauptmann et al. [63] with TRECVID news video conclude that low-quality feature detectors, if there are thousands of them, can together provide high accuracy results for semantic video retrieval. CBIR with a few thousand concepts detected with minimal accuracy of 10% MAP are likely to provide high accuracy results, comparable to text retrieval on the Web, in a typical broadcast news collection [63].

The automatic visual concept classifiers typically make use of supervised learning techniques. A number of positive and negative examples are given for a concept such as "road." An underlying feature set of color histograms, Canny edges, SIFT features, Gabor filters, and other encodings for color, edges, textures, and shape describe every example. Learning algorithms construct a statistical model based on the examples' features to allow subsequent classification of unlabeled data with that concept. Supervised learning dominates the work of TRECVID researchers investigating automatic feature classification (see the online TRECVID reports through the years for more details). A continuing research question is whether the classifiers built with a particular set of training data will generalize, e.g., will classifiers built from American broadcast news work with Arabic news, or will classifiers built from news work just as well against documentaries? With supervised learning, labeled training data provide domain knowledge about a concept such as "road." With unsupervised structure discovery, no training examples are necessary; however, these approaches work best when the domain knowledge comes through limiting the input genre. For example, interesting game states can be revealed without supervision, by limiting the automated processing to only sports videos [45].

In concluding this section, consider two of the successful automatic visual classifiers: text and face detection. Text detection is the first step in video optical character recognition (VOCR), where text areas are detected, passed to commercial OCR systems, and metadata is then output in the form of text [65]. VOCR works with both scene text where letters, numerals, and symbols are shown on signs, for instance, as well as overlaid text placed there in postproduction (e.g., the names shown underneath experts in broadcast news). Figure 2.7 shows the Informedia text detection step of VOCR against a number of different shots, with skewed scene text and low-contrast overlaid text being missed, and the Capitol's columns being mistaken as text.

VOCR receives continued attention from corporations such as SRI International, which developed ConTEXTract to better detect text in skewed nonplanar scene text and to deal with a variety of fonts and languages [66].

Along with text detection, face detection is another success story for visual processing, with Figure 2.7 showing the output of the Schneiderman face detector [67] used by Informedia in its video processing. This detector has received a 2008 computer vision society award for withstanding the test of time, and led to the creation of a company where you can try out the current version of the face detector yourself [68].

In summary, image processing for video can detect low-level syntactic attributes such as color, texture, or shape. In addition, higher-order features such as face or text can be detected, with work ongoing by researchers and evaluated through forums such as TRECVID for hundreds of other

FIGURE 2.7: Red boxes illustrating Informedia automatic text detection against video shots (before subsequent steps to merge smaller detected areas into lines of text), with yellow boxes bounding the detected faces.

features such as building, road, police, or animal. Knowing the source video's genre can considerably improve feature classification accuracy, e.g., only trying to detect a soccer goal for soccer video, or only detecting news studio and advertisements for broadcast news with embedded advertisements. The temporal flow of a video, as opposed to a static image, allows for temporally dependent metadata to be generated as well. The most common examples are camera motion (e.g., pan, tilt, zoom) and object motion (e.g., static or something moving and the direction of motion). Looking at differences in metadata across time allows for a long source video to be decomposed into a temporal series of shots, with simple color histogram differences providing for more than 90% accuracy in shot detection [33].

2.3   LANGUAGE PROCESSING

If text is available from VOCR, ASR, and other aural and visual processing steps representing their output as text, then such text can be further refined through named entity detection to identify places, organizations, and people. BBN has commercialized the processing of ASR-quality transcription (i.e., transcripts with some error) using hidden Markov models (HMM) to classify text produced from speech recognition into named entities such as people, places, or organizations [69]. Informedia similarly uses HMMs to detect named entities, as illustrated in Figure 2.8.

When such processing is armed with additional information such as a gazetteer that gives latitude and longitude location attributes for place names, then places in the metadata can be geographically located on maps. Informedia mapping of place names to gazetteer entries is titled geocoding because it uses temporal information from ASR, speech-aligned text, and VOCR appearance times of text to note when the place text appears in the video.

If an ambiguous location such as "Rochester" appears surrounded by more text in the immediate temporal neighborhood discussing "New York" frequently, then that evidence for "Rochester,

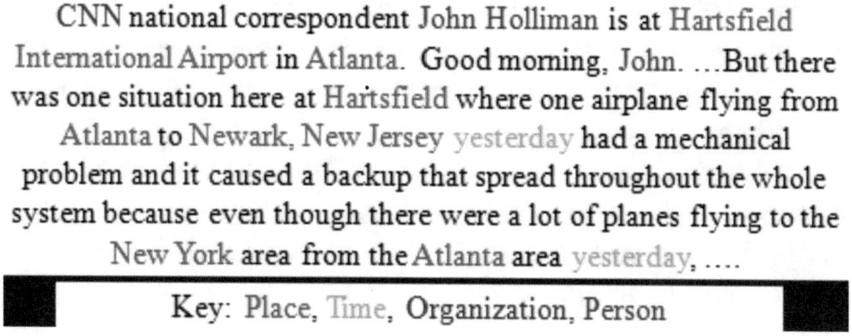

CNN national correspondent John Holliman is at Hartsfield International Airport in Atlanta. Good morning, John. …But there was one situation here at Hartsfield where one airplane flying from Atlanta to Newark, New Jersey yesterday had a mechanical problem and it caused a backup that spread throughout the whole system because even though there were a lot of planes flying to the New York area from the Atlanta area yesterday, ….

Key: Place, Time, Organization, Person

FIGURE 2.8: Example use of automatic named entity detection to organize text metadata into place, person, and other entity categories, which can receive additional specialized processing.

New York" over "Rochester, Minnesota" is used to provide a confidence toward the Rochester, NY, gazetteer entry. Silence points and durations help mark sentence boundaries, with text evidence within the sentence weighted higher than further out. Similarly, black frames and shot boundaries delimit the evidence visually: text within a shot or not crossing black frames used internationally in many broadcasts to mark advertisements is weighted higher than more distant text. Geocoding shows an example of how language processing and disambiguation is aided through multimodal temporal cues.

Similarly, when armed with an authority file for names such as the Library of Congress Authorities, multiple expressions of a person's name can be redirected to that person's authority record. Extra sources of information can reduce the ambiguity of the text and allow higher orders of specificity in the text metadata.

2.4   REFLECTIONS/EXERCISES

Based on the discussion on the Panofsky–Shatford matrix of picture subjects and the overview of automated processing techniques, consider the following issues:

1. Suppose you are tasked to automatically classify multimedia objects as frightening, calming, or neutral. How would you go about this exercise?

2. Suppose an ASR engine never transcribed articles correctly, i.e., words such as "a," "an," and "the." Would the output still be useful? What if it only transcribed nouns correctly? What would be missing if you ran ASR on news, but the only vocabulary it knew were the words in the *Wall Street Journal* from 1990 to 2005?

3. Test out multiple image search services on the Web, e.g., Google Image Search (http://images.google.com/), ALIPR (http://alipr.com/), picsearch (http://www.picsearch.com/). Try a range of queries from simple to compound, e.g., "red car," "red car white bricks," "red car in front of white bricks." Look in a magazine for photos and see whether you could locate visually similar photos using these services. Now switch to specific queries, e.g., "Tony Blair" or "Washington Monument." Are these easier for the Web image search services to satisfy? Why or why not?

4. Test face detection, e.g., at Pittsburgh Pattern Recognition (http://demo.pittpatt.com/). Test how well images-to-text services work for those that let you input your own images (e.g., ALIPR). How might such services let you categorize video at various levels of the Jaimes classification pyramid?

CHAPTER 3

Refinement of Automatic Metadata

There are numerous approaches that can be taken to refine automatically produced metadata. One could manually identify the input type and throw away classification that is nonsensical, e.g., news studio classificaton from classroom lecture videos. One could invest additional human labor to correct automatic speech recognition (ASR) text into a more accurate transcription. The human correction process itself can serve as a form of relevance feedback that can perhaps improve the original metadata creation programs. For example, by showing thumbnails of shots marked with a feature such as "road" and having a human work through the shots and identify those that were incorrectly tagged, the computer can pick up additional training data that through active learning may lead to a better "road" detector [70]. This form of relevance feedback works if the user's additional positive and negative examples help to reduce one or both of false positives (mislabeling a nonroad shot as road) and false negatives (incorrectly labeling a road shot as not road).

There is a paradigm in computer vision, interactive computer vision, that acknowledges the difficulties in many computer vision tasks and encourages human guidance and input to complete the tasks. This paradigm, endorsed by Shum et al. [71], involves human interaction as an integral part of the vision algorithm. The same paradigm applies here, given the contributing role that computer vision work plays in multimedia information automated processing as well. Rather than force the impossible, that automatic metadata must be 100% accurate, human correction can be encouraged, streamlined, and mined to support an ever-improving set of metadata for a collection, as with the active learning road detector mentioned above.

This section gives examples of three other means of improving the automated metadata aside from human correction: using more computation, multimodal redundancy, and leveraging context.

3.1   COMPUTATIONALLY INTENSIVE APPROACHES

Larger, more complete knowledge sources can potentially produce more accurate classifiers. A lexicon covering all spoken words for a library would eliminate ASR out of vocabulary problems, and if armed with a complete acoustic model and language model (see Figure 2.5), the overall quality of

ASR benefits as well. Similarly, a lexicon armed with more labeled examples of roads and nonroads can lead to a better road detector. However, there are limits on benefits from larger knowledge source sizes. For ASR, the issues in Figure 2.4 can downgrade results even with a huge lexicon, and the differences in output quality as shown in Figure 2.6 are due to factors simply beyond the out-of-vocabulary issue addressable through the lexicon. For a road detector, if the underlying syntactic features for "road" are inappropriate, e.g., suppose they only include color and no edges or textures, then regardless of how large the training set is, the road detector will perform poorly because of a mismatch between the features and the road concept.

The Lucas–Kanade method for optical flow estimation [72] is a computationally expensive but accurate way of assessing camera or object motion by looking at pixel-by-pixel differences between image frames. The method is expensive in that every pair of sequential frames in a video could be compared for highest precision, and every pixel considered in each comparison. The results are very accurate depictions of object motion and camera motion. Consider Figure 3.1, which shows a visual rendering of the optical flow tracing. The technique works well in distinguishing something moving in the scene versus the camera moving. In these examples, the polar bear is static but the camera is panning upward, whereas the camaflouged soldier in front of the visually busy backdrop is moving to the right.

Template-driven approaches also produce higher accuracy at the expense of computation. Consider the problem of face detection as shown in Figure 2.7. A template-based approach (see Yang et al. [73] for this and other face detection methods) runs a pattern of two eyes, a nose, and a mouth at a given size, say a postage stamp, across every area of each video frame, starting in the upper left and working down to the lower right, identifying all matches to the stamp-sized template. The template can then be scaled slightly larger, and run across the whole video again, with the repeating process having greater accuracy by scaling to various candidate sizes. With further computation, more accuracy can be achieved in finding rotated faces by rotating the template as

FIGURE 3.1: Visual rendering of optical flow for images 0.5 seconds apart, pixel-by-pixel trace showing numerous vertical traces for camera vertical pan, whereas the right sequence has numerous pinpricks and only some horizontal lines indicating an object moving to the right, rather than a camera pan.

well, and running it again at various sizes across the different positions in each frame of the video. All matches to the template will be identified across various scales, translations, and rotations, at the expense of doing numerous matches against the template.

3.2   TEMPORAL AND MULTIMODAL REDUNDANCY

Two forms of redundancy can help improve automatic metadata creation. The first is temporal redundancy, the fact that the visual information in a video changes only slightly from frame to frame (e.g., for NTSC video, only slightly from one frame to the next, which occurs 1/30 of a second later). This redundancy allows optical flow to work well (Figure 3.1), at the expense of computations running across every pixel. Frame-to-frame redundancy with some motion in the camera, the scene, or both can be leveraged to supply video "super resolution," sharpening detail in objects such as license plates to make them legible. One commercial offering of such technology is the Ikena Reveal product offering of MotionDSP [74]. The same redundancy allows template-based detectors such as text detection to become more accurate.

For the Informedia video optical character recognition (VOCR) process, the first step of identifying text areas is rather noisy, as shown in Figure 3.2. The top right image shows numerous areas detected as text, shown in white. The next image, from a half second later, shows its text candidate

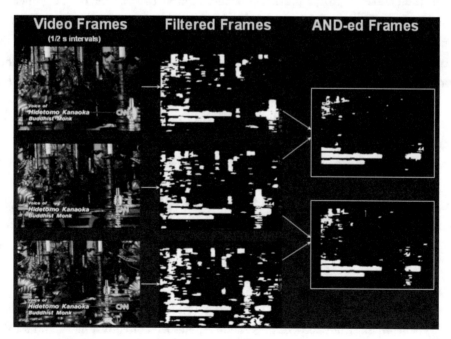

FIGURE 3.2: Leveraging video visual redundancy across time to improve the accuracy of detected text areas, shown in white.

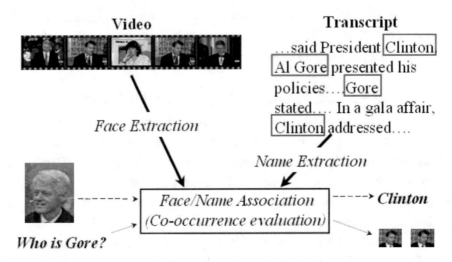

FIGURE 3.3: Name-It association: tagging faces (from visual processing) with proper names (from aural/text processing).

areas, which when and'ed with the previous matches reduces the candidate set significantly. Continuing this merging of text candidate areas in frames across the same shot results in a final detected set with greater accuracy, obtained by leveraging video redundancy over time. Through the use of context, e.g., the heuristic that readable text has a minimum size and that it will run in horizontal lengths for English broadcasts, allows the candidate set to be further reduced to just the horizontal detected bars where text actually occurs in the source video.

The redundancy between the aural information and visual information can also be leveraged to improve specificity. Visual processing can detect faces. Aural information through ASR results in text, which—following named entity tagging—produces a list of proper names. Those names can be associated with text to allow "Person X" identification, i.e., identifying that a particular face is Bill Clinton or Al Gore [75, 76]. This "Name-It" classification of Informedia is illustrated in Figure 3.3.

Similar tagging can be done to process outdoor shots with buildings and label them with locations [32], increasing the specificity of tags through aural, visual, and language processing.

3.3   LEVERAGING CONTEXT

The National Institute of Standards and Technology (NIST) TREC Video Retrieval Evaluation (TRECVID) benchmarks from 2002 through 2006 emphasized broadcast news, and for that genre it became clear through the years that anchorperson shots and news studio shots in general rarely contributed to information needs (rather, the field footage held the visually interesting content).

The anchorperson and studio shots, through face detection, face size and location, color and shape cues, and edges/lines cues, could be easily detected to a high degree of accuracy. Although the anchorperson might change, the framing of the anchorperson in the camera typically did not, so TRECVID participants could successfully find anchorperson and studio shots for use not only in automatic and interactive querying, but also to detect higher-order concepts (e.g., reporter in the field is a face but not an anchorperson), and decomposition processing (a news story is typically bracketed by anchorperson shots and/or commercials [77]). Context-specific processing can reduce the meaningful text detection areas of Figure 3.2, with more reduction possible through the availability of administrative metadata (e.g., the broadcaster and broadcast date for news). Given such administrative information, network logos can be removed, and scrolling text lines independent of the visuals removed based on where given broadcasters place such information.

This type of tuning by context is precisely how sports video processing can achieve the 90% or higher success rates published in multimedia conferences for events such as scoring. For example, armed with contextual knowledge that a scoring event is followed by the omnipresent numeric score changing in a particular area of the visual given a broadcaster, the detector for scoring event can focus on the score area and numbers changing, rather than the deeper and more difficult processing of the field of play.

Context can come from general rules (e.g., text appearing at minimal sizes in horizontal runs regarding Figure 3.2), input genres (anchorperson shots appear in news), or broadcast specifics (known visual areas for score listings or network logos). Context can also come from the history of interaction with the multimedia corpus by a human user. In the remainder of this lecture, we will use two video data sets for illustration:

- NIST TRECVID 2006 broadcast news test set: 165 hours of U.S., Arabic, and Chinese news sources, 5923 story segments, 146,328 shots.
- Life oral history interviews from The HistoryMakers recorded from 1993 through August 2005: 913 hours, 400 interviewees, 18,254 story segments (1 shot per segment).

One of the early Informedia user studies looked at the difficulty of representing documentary footage with a single thumbnail image. With a thumbnail per shot, a documentary story segment has numerous candidates to represent it, and user query context, i.e., what is being searched for, can identify which thumbnail will work best. This query-based thumbnail selection results in a more satisfying interface to the end user offering greater utility [78].

The query-based thumbnail selection process is illustrated here using TRECVID 2006 news data. Suppose the information need is helicopters. A matching news story has a number of shots, typical because Informedia processing over a decade has found news shots to average roughly

2.2 seconds in length. One such story with its storyboard of thumbnails, one per shot in sequential order, is shown in Figure 3.4.

The two red notches in the fourth and fifth thumbnails on the top row show the times where "helicopter" matched (against VOCR text and/or spoken narrative). In choosing a single thumbnail to represent the story, the highest-scoring shot with a match (i.e., with a notch) is chosen, with a news context rule also in place to pick nonanchor shots wherever possible. The result is the selection of the helicopter image for use in a story segment view, illustrated in Figure 3.5.

Query context can be used not only for filtering as in Figure 3.5 but also for construction (e.g., for constructing a set of common text phrases from speech transcripts following a query against a video set). The original metadata gives a set of text per video segment. A query returns a set of video segments. At runtime following the query, the common text phrases for that video set can be presented as metadata enhancing collection understanding, a topic that will be revisited later in this lecture. With respect to the HistoryMakers corpus, consider Figure 3.6: a query on "baseball" returns 414 segments, with the common text phrases such as "Jackie Robinson" shown at left. The user filters to the 20 baseball stories mentioning "Kansas City," and the common text phrases for those 20 are now more detailed for that chosen focus, e.g., listing "Kansas City Monarchs," which was the name of that city's Negro League baseball team. Testing with numerous universities' history and African American Studies students in 2007 and 2008 has shown that this text-based collection level view, driven by context, is well received and used frequently.

One final example of context is using appropriate sources of authoritative outside knowledge. Clearly, the text in Figure 3.6 could be improved, from simple redundancy removal to listing a place only once with accurate containment based on a gazetteer appropriate for the corpus, e.g., "Kansas City, MO, USA." Similarly, the knowledge sources for ASR (Figure 2.5) can be tuned to match expected input data.

FIGURE 3.4: Storyboard (one thumbnail per shot) for a news segment matching "helicopter" in shots 4 and 5.

FIGURE 3.5: Segment view (one thumbnail per story segment) for a set of five videos matching "helicopter" (see also Figure 3.4).

Returning to automated VOCR, consider Figure 3.7, where the white shirt–dark tie crossing interfered with the letters "TY" in "COUNTY" and caused the VOCR output to incorrectly state "COUNA." If context were applied to accumulate statistical likelihoods of word phrases, this error could be corrected. In this example, COUNA could be flagged as a likely error because it does not occur in the lexicon, and mining the open web for sequences of the form "Los Angeles" followed by a word followed by "Sheriff" would turn up a few candidates of which "County" would be syntactically close to "COUNA" and chosen as the better output for the VOCR process.

Figure 3.7, of course, shows the best case, with a single poor entry being replaced by a candidate easy to decipher from the open web. If the proper name "Sherman Block" had been misrecognized, it may not have been noticed or may not be as easy to clean up, unless additional contextual cues were used.

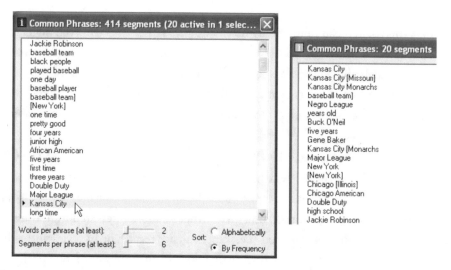

FIGURE 3.6: Collection-level metadata of common text phrases for 414 HistoryMakers story segments returned from "baseball" query (left), and the common text for the 20 baseball segments discussing Kansas City (right).

FIGURE 3.7: Example of VOCR process producing incorrect output "COUNA" that could be cleaned up through statistical processing for "Los Angeles <blank> Sheriff" candidates.

For news, this could mean mining only news web sites rather than the Web in general, mining the same period as the VOCR'd broadcast in question leveraging from administrative metadata, or mining just that particular broadcaster's web site. The lesson from this portion of the lecture is that automated metadata will have errors, some of which can be corrected by leveraging context. The more appropriate the contextual cues, the more likely the errors can be corrected in meaningful ways.

3.4 USER-CONTROLLED PRECISION-RECALL TRADE-OFF

Automatically produced descriptors will have errors. Both ASR and visual concept processing, for example, are far from perfect, and over the years the Informedia research team has found that, depending on audience, corpus, and task, users will either be more interested in finding all the relevant occurrences for an information need (i.e., emphasizing recall), or in reviewing only relevant occurrences (i.e., emphasizing precision). Rather than lock in an emphasis on one or the other with automated processing, the metadata can carry with it confidence information supporting dynamic adjustment of precision versus recall by the end user at runtime. Two examples are given illustrating the use of such confidence attributes on descriptors.

Consider a location identifier from spoken dialog. Instead of removing possible but unlikely candidates, which would reduce the false positive rate and increase precision, a location such as "Hampton, NH" could be left in as a label for a story with Hampton weakly tagged as a location and New Hampshire mentioned somewhere in the story but temporally distant from the "Hampton" mention. The location could be given low confidence. Users armed with means of searching maps could decide for themselves whether increased recall at the expense of precision was desired. Figure 3.8 shows results of a New Hampshire query against The HistoryMakers. The topmost set is more precise, but omits details about a match to Tilton, NH. The bottommost set includes Tilton, but also includes Hampton and Littleton, which are false positives (in these stories, they refer to people and not cities).

As a second example, shot-based confidence filtering led to a number of studies and interface experiments with dynamic query sliders [79, 80]. Over time, the most efficient interface displayed the query slider in an "off" state and let the user either keep or drop the listed visual concept, which would set up the widget's slider at one end or the other for further interaction. Shot-based filtering is extremely important for shot-based information retrieval tasks such as those studied with TRECVID because of the vast number of shots available even after the query. For example, consider Figure 3.9, which shows a query of disaster terms against the TRECVID 2006 corpus. The result set has 354 segments, 10,054 shots, but only 1204 shots temporally near to one of the five query term matches (against spoken narrative and/or VOCR text).

If the user were interested in outdoor setting shots of buildings but no identifiable people from this query, perhaps to reuse as a backdrop for another disaster story, they could make use of

FIGURE 3.8: Example of user control over location metadata precision to return different video sets from a map query (NH).

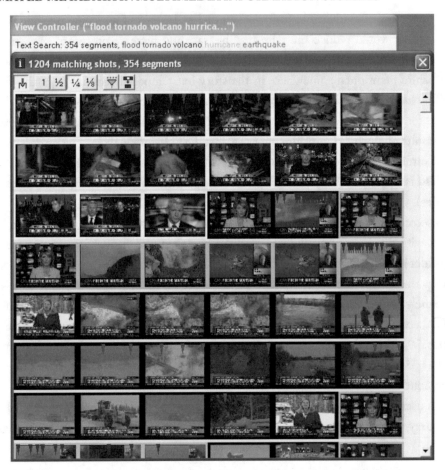

FIGURE 3.9: Storyboard of 1204 matching shots following query on "flood tornado volcano hurricane earthquake."

visual concept filters to drop faces, keep outdoors, and keep buildings, adjusting confidences on these sliders until the desired quality and count in the shown storyboard meets the user's needs. Figure 3.10 shows the result of applying such query sliders against the shots shown in Figure 3.9.

As these figures illustrate, rather than classify a shot as a boolean "is outdoors or not," the shot has an outdoors confidence in a $[0, 1]$ range that can then be shown in the histograms within the query slider of Figure 3.10 and manipulated by users based on their information needs and task requirements. Revisiting a point made at the start of this metadata refinement section, the user can mark shots that are incorrect, e.g., the blue graphic shot at the end of the top row in Figure 3.10 being incorrectly classified as both outdoor and building. Passing these marked shots back to the automatic classification system can improve the accuracy of subsequent outdoor and building classi-

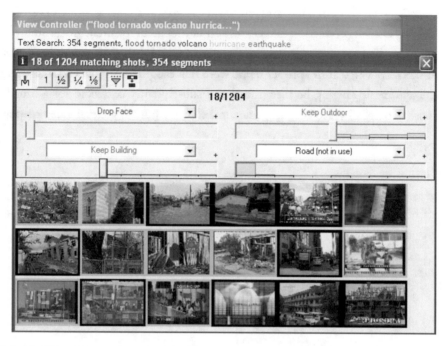

FIGURE 3.10: User-driven control of precision-recall, adjusting sliders to keep primarily outdoor building shots with no faces, reducing 1204 shots to a very manageable set of 18 shots.

fiers through active learning [70]. In this case, passing enough shots like the noted blue graphic will teach the system that computer-generated graphics should not be considered as outdoor.

3.5   REFLECTIONS/EXERCISES

1. Metadata can be corrected through human review, as is done for the HistoryMakers data set used in examples here, where speech transcription was manually refined. Such correction is tedious and produces its own set of errors. Consider clean-up tasks for different metadata types, e.g., outdoor shot detection, ASR transcription, and specific location detection (in text and in visuals). How would you employ a human archivist in correcting such data, and what tools could you see aiding the process?

2. Human computation and games with a purpose (GWAP) are offered as one potential solution toward the semantic gap of multimedia information retrieval [81]. Specifically, the ESP Game allows images to be tagged with text, and Peekaboom allows objects to be identified within images, with these and other GWAP examples available for use at http://

www.gwap.com. Try out a few and report on the pros and cons of using GWAP as a means of driving human production and correction of metadata for multimedia archives.

3. Figure 3.7 illustrates a misrecognized word "COUNA" that could be corrected into "COUNTY." What if the proper name were misrecognized? How can mistakes in proper name automatic tagging be recognized and subsequently corrected for a broadcast news corpus? A baseball video corpus? A documentary corpus? A general video corpus?

·   ·   ·   ·

CHAPTER 4

Multimedia Surrogates

To illustrate earlier sections, multimedia surrogates of thumbnails and storyboards have been shown in figures. In information retrieval, the term "document surrogate" is used to label information that serves as the representation for the full document, such as a title, abstract, table of contents, set of keywords, or combinations of these descriptors. For a multimedia document with audio and/or video and a temporal dimension, a multimedia surrogate labels the set of text, image, audio, and/or video that can serve as a condensed representation for the full multimedia document.

Video summaries have many purposes, overviewed well by Taskiran et al. [82] and including the following: intriguing the user to watch the whole video (movie trailers), quickly deciding if the program is worth watching (electronic program guide), locating specific regions of interest (lecture overview), collapsing highly redundant footage into the subset with important information (surveillance executive summary). For most applications, multimedia summaries mainly serve two functions, again drawing from [82]: an indicative function, where the summary is used to indicate what topics of information are contained in the original multimedia document; and the informative function, where the summaries are used to cover the information in the source as much as possible, subject to the summary length. This lecture focuses on multimedia surrogates meant for indicative summaries, i.e., the description and assessment of video surrogates meant to help users better judge the relevance of the source program for their task at hand.

4.1 VIDEO SURROGATE EXAMPLES

Traditionally, old format multimedia objects in libraries, such as analog audiotapes and videotapes, have been described with text-only surrogates, typically a short abstract or perhaps just a title or brief list of keywords. Through automated processing, any administrative or provenance text metadata can be supplemented with text from processes such as automatic speech recognition and video optical character recognition. Through named entity detection, people and place name specifics can be emphasized in creating short text surrogates such as titles for multimedia documents. A text title that includes a bit of structural metadata, namely, the duration of the multimedia document, has been in use in Informedia since it was first fielded in schools in the mid-1990s. Unlike text corpora, however, the multimedia has much more information to draw from and can have a richer form of presentation besides text only.

One common purpose of a multimedia surrogate is to provide an indicative function while also allowing quick visual navigation within a whole, such as a table of contents, for which synchronized metadata and a temporal overview such as the storyboard (Figure 3.4) is well suited. The single thumbnail representation per document (video segment) is more compact (Figure 3.5), and, when the thumbnail is chosen based on query context, can be more satisfying than and as equally efficient as text labels [78].

TREC Video Retrieval Evaluation (TRECVID) has had a shot detection task charting the progress of automatic shot detection since 2001, and has shown it to be one of the most realizable tasks for video processing with accuracy in excess of 90% [33]. With accurate shot detection, selecting a frame within the shot to represent it as a thumbnail, i.e., a single bitmap image, is straightforward because there is visual homogeneity within the frames in a shot. Because shot starts and ends may be clouded with digital video effects such as dissolves and fades, the standard practice is to select a frame from the middle of the shot to use as the shot's thumbnail representation. The thumbnail images for each shot can be arranged into a single chronological display, a storyboard surrogate, which captures the visual flow of a video document. Storyboards serve as an effective visual table of contents and date back to the advent of digital video. Numerous commercial and research systems such as CAETI, EUROMEDIA, Físchlár, VideoLogger, Open Video, and of course Informedia have implementations of storyboards showing shot thumbnails arranged in chronological order [83].

Text can be an important component of multimedia surrogates. Indeed, Ding et al. [3] found that video surrogates including both text and imagery are more effective than either modality alone. An eye-tracking study was conducted to look at digital video surrogates composed of text and three thumbnail images to represent each document, and it was observed that participants looked at and fixated on text far more than pictures [84]. They used the text as an anchor from which to make judgments about the list of results. The value of using text and imagery together in video surrogates was confirmed in an Informedia user study that specifically examined the questions of text layouts and lengths in storyboards [85]. Twenty-five university students and staff members participated in an experiment using a fact-finding task against a news video corpus, where dependent measures included correctness, time to complete the task, and subjective satisfaction. In news video, information is conveyed both through visuals (especially field footage) and audio (such as the script read by the newscaster), so a mixed presentation of both synchronized shot images and transcript text extracts was expected to offer benefits over image-only storyboards (see Figure 4.1 for tested treatments).

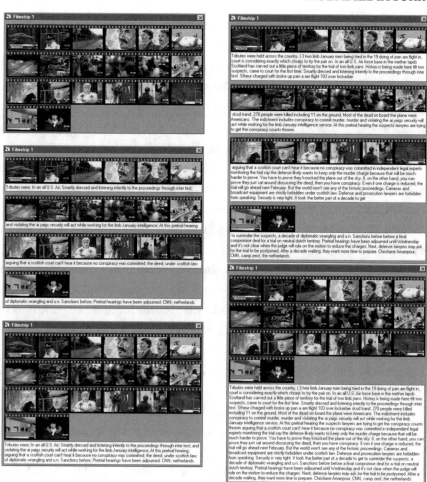

FIGURE 4.1: Tested treatments for text with storyboard: aligned or not, brief, full, or no text, in Informedia study [85].

Significant differences in performance time and satisfaction were found in the study [85]. Storyboard surrogates clearly improved with text, and participants favored the interleaved presentation. If interleaving is done in conjunction with text reduction, to better preserve and represent the time association between lines of text, imagery, and their affiliated video sequence, then a storyboard with great utility for information assessment and navigation can be constructed. That is, the transcript text should be time-aligned with thumbnail rows in the storyboard, and then reduced to a set of basic phrases important to the particular query context. Further studies regarding the alignment of imagery with text or audio keywords in video surrogates have been conducted in the context of the Open Video project [86, 87]. The study of Christel and Warmack [85] also found that assembling surrogates from phrases (longer chunks) works better than assembling from words (shorter chunks).

This latter conclusion was also reached in an assessment of a playable video surrogate: a video skim of audio and visual information with the play duration 7.5 times shorter than the target video. The assessment found that the skim was more effective if composed of longer 5-second phrase-aligned audio chunks than shorter 2.5-second chunks [1]. The video was sampled at evenly spaced intervals (e.g., extract 5 seconds, skip 32.5, repeat), with the audio slid temporally to align on relative silence (phrase) boundaries. Playable video summaries have received renewed attention from the TRECVID community in its BBC Rushes Summarization Task, looking at indicative and informative summaries that have at most 4% of the source length in 2007, and 2% of the source length in 2008. Although storyboards are the most frequently used surrogate with video libraries seen today, they are not universally viewed as being sufficient. On the contrary, a 2007 workshop involving the BBC [88] witnessed discussion over the shortcomings of storyboards and the need for playable, temporal summaries and other forms of video surrogates for review and interactive interfaces for control. A BBC participant stated that we have had storyboards for more 10 years now (more, if we go back to Mills et al.'s [89] work with storyboards and QuickTime interfaces), and that industry is looking to the multimedia research community for the latest advances. Playable video surrogates are reported in detail in that workshop [88] and its 2008 equivalent, and so will not be emphasized here. Past work on visual skims has noted (1) the importance of synchronization between modalities; and (2) the value of multiple modalities, e.g., audio and video, when the source information has content in those channels (as is true for documentaries and news, and often not true for surveillance). Also worth noting is the effectiveness of a straightforward video skim generation process, needing only a subsampling of the source video's frames. Wildemuth and her coauthors [90] found that for produced documentary materials, fast-forward surrogates with accelerated playback can be effective. They tested 32×, 64×, 128×, and 256× video surrogates (video that samples every 32, 64, 128, or 256 frames, with no audio component) with four target documentary video segments. They conclude from an empirical study with 45 participants and six measures of human performance that 64× is the recommended speed for the fast-forward surrogate, supporting good performance and user satisfaction [90]. For BBC rush materials with much redundancy due to repeated takes, 50× worked nearly as well as 25× and offered much greater efficiency [91], with the contribution of an audio component to the playable 50× summary still an open area of investigation [92].

Showing distribution and density of match terms is useful, and can naturally be added to a storyboard (notches in Figures 3.4 and 3.9) or a video player's play progress bar. The interface representation for the match term can be used to navigate quickly to that point in the video where the match occurs. The overview can show whether the multimedia document has few or many matches, to what terms, and concentrated or spread uniformly in time. This surrogate feature is made possible by the temporal dimension of the multimedia document (e.g., so that time maps to horizontal placement), and having metadata all contain a time reference, i.e., all metadata is synchronized to its source multimedia document. In subsequent searches on imagery, text, named entities, etc., the matching metadata can then be returned as well as the times where matches occurred.

4.2   SURROGATES FOR COLLECTIONS OF VIDEO

Users lost in the space of a single-hour multimedia document may sacrifice an hour to locate material of interest, but users lost in the space of a thousand-hour video set cannot possibly find what they are after with reasonable performance, speed, or satisfaction: the utility of surrogates for summarizing sets of video increases dramatically. In this discussion centering on Informedia, the multimedia document is a video story segment, manually delineated for The HistoryMakers, automatically delineated for the TRECVID 2006 news set.

As one example has already shown, the storyboard surrogate can be extended to represent not only shots from a single segment, but shots from multiple segments in a video set, as shown in Figure 3.9. The storyboard coupled with dynamic query sliders on visual concepts allows for visually driven exploration of large video sets.

As noted by Hughes et al. [84] and seen with the HistoryMakers humanities users [93], users of multimedia repositories are often drawn to text first, not visuals, and some corpora such as the HistoryMakers oral histories have a wealth of text material from transcripts and fewer shots to work with in storyboards. Text-centric collection surrogates have value, of which one is the common text view of phrases for a video set. The phrases can be organized simply by frequency of occurrence or alphabetically, and filtered based on coverage of the video set and number of words per phrase; this view is illustrated in Figure 3.7. Another text-centric view is a nested tree browser showing the decomposition of original video submission into story segments. For The HistoryMakers, this view lets the user see the interviewee, interview session, and interview story segment for each member of a set of video. Using the same 414 segments from baseball shown in Figure 3.6, the Nested Lists view is shown in the upper right of Figure 4.2. The 414 stories come from 173 individuals, with Ernie Banks providing 31 of those stories including the highlighted one from 1948.

The Informedia timeline surrogate plots video segments against a horizontal axis, with the y axis as search service relevance score by default in Figure 4.2, but modifiable to be duration or some other information attribute of interest. For the HistoryMakers, each story segment may have zero to many time references, and each time reference may be precise (June 1, 1968) or fuzzy (August 1968 or "the 1960s"), with a strategy to show every time reference that intersects the active time region of the timeline, e.g., broad references to decades or centuries are not lost as one zooms into years [94]. For news, the timeline plot is accomplished through only provenance metadata giving the broadcast date, with the plot communicating when the news was aired. For example, Figure 4.3 shows a timeline

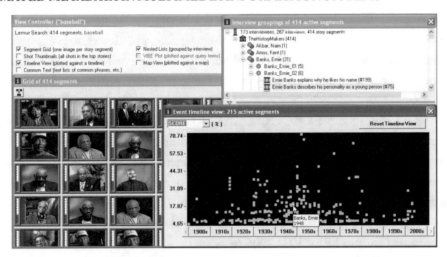

FIGURE 4.2: Segment Grid, Timeline, and Nested Lists surrogates showing different emphases in collection-level view of 414 HistoryMakers story segments.

view of the same disaster query used in Figure 3.9 for TRECVID 2006, whose corpus is limited to November and December 2005 broadcasts. Even the small time window shows a spike of activity on November 24, which corresponds to the eruption of the Galeras volcano in Colombia.

A fully dynamic, interactive multimedia surrogate within the Informedia interface is the Visual Information Browsing Environment (VIBE) view developed at the University of Pittsburgh [95]. VIBE represents query terms as nodes. Documents are represented by plotted rectangles suspended within the surface bounded by the query terms. The internal representation of a document

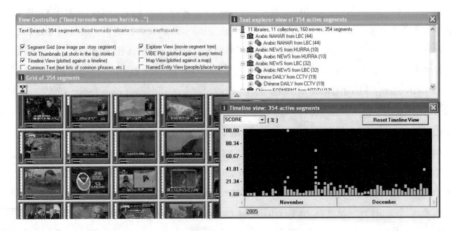

FIGURE 4.3: Segment Grid, Timeline, and Nested Lists surrogates showing different emphases in collection-level view of 354 news story segments from TRECVID 2006 test set.

is a weighted term vector according to the search engine producing the video set, and the interface position of the document is calculated as the vector sum of the components indicated by the query terms. For the same query in Figure 4.3, the VIBE view is shown in Figure 4.4, which shows at first glance a strong relationship between "flood" and "hurricane." Through quick interaction of moving the query term anchor points, the user can see the documents reposition themselves in the VIBE plot, and along with tooltips giving counts, discover that there are 20 segments matching volcano, that 18 of those 20 only match volcano without discussing the other disasters, the other two both mention earthquake, and one of the 20 also mentions hurricane. In addition, by showing the VIBE view and Timeline view (Figure 4.3) together for the video set, information brushing can be used to show relationships between the views through color. Mousing over the plot point representing the 18 documents in VIBE that match only "volcano" (point right at volcano) will color most of the stories vertically lined up at the November 24 point in the timeline, showing a direct time relationship between "volcano" and a specific date.

Greater specificity in the metadata, i.e., teasing out named entities from text descriptors, allows for views tailored to names, locations, and organizations. Locations obviously plot well on maps, and two map views, one emphasizing U.S. states and the other the world, are shown in Figure 4.5. As discussed with VIBE and Timeline brushing, interactions with the Map view can dynamically update the other views, and updating the other views can dynamically update the map. The various views, or multimedia surrogates for a set of video documents, act in coordination with each other, so together they paint a picture of the contents of the set of video. These views can be controlled with query sliders, shown in Figure 4.5 with the baseball "states" view color-coded and controlled by a Score slider, and the disaster world view controlled by a broadcast date slider.

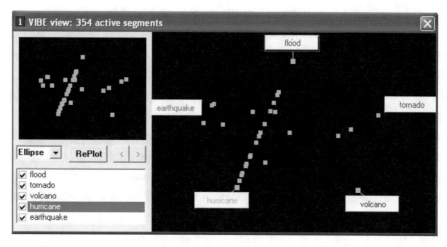

FIGURE 4.4: VIBE surrogate for 354 story segments of Figure 4.3.

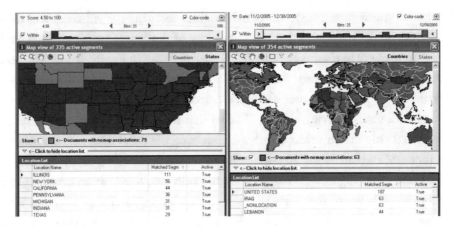

FIGURE 4.5: Map view for baseball query against HistoryMakers (left) and disaster query from Figure 4.4 and earlier against November 2005 news in TRECVID 2006 data set.

Early Informedia work on a multimedia collage emphasizing important visuals and text on a map showed the summarization value of presenting such information to the user [96], but also showed that layout issues, especially with thumbnails, were an issue. Putting thumbnails directly on the map obscured the map regions. By having surrogates that specialize in showcasing different attributes—e.g., Shot Thumbnails (storyboards) for visual content, and Maps for geographic distribution—that are each in their own window, yet coordinated, the user can more easily interact with and appreciate the summary of a multimedia collage composed of various views without occlusion.

The named entities can be plotted in their own view, using shape to distinguish people, organizations, and places. As with Common Text, the Named Entity view can filter contents based on coverage in the video set, e.g., a named entity must appear in at least five video documents to be plotted. As with the match notches shown on storyboards, synchronization metadata is critically important, because named entities are connected only if they appear within a short enough time window to each other. Figure 4.6 shows the named entity view for the disaster query and TRECVID 2006 data set, centered on named entities tied temporally to Katrina and listing just the entities automatically tagged as organizations. The Named Entity View offers a key interactive feature: the ability to produce context-rich video summaries, with the user selecting the context. Here, the user chooses to center on "Katrina," and play all of the six segments associating Federal Emergency Management Agency (FEMA) with Katrina. This user action leads to a playable video skim, a temporal surrogate, which focuses on just that context, FEMA as related to Katrina, in the player shown at the upper right. Unlike the fast-forward surrogates discussed earlier for documentaries and BBC rushes [90, 91, 92], these skims play more smoothly, are more satisfying to users, and have perfectly synchronized audio because they are a series of extracts from the original source

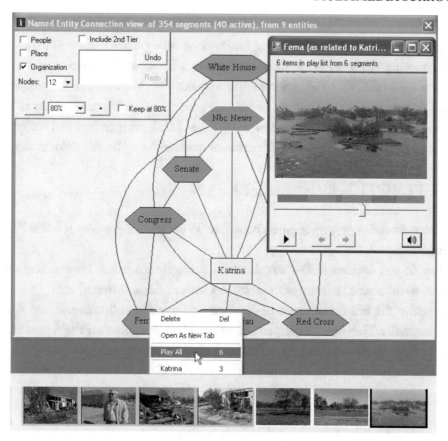

FIGURE 4.6: Named entity view of organizations discussed with Katrina (top), enabling the user to drill down to play just a temporal summary of certain relationships, here showing the six video document snippets tying FEMA to Katrina; bottom view shows contents of Shot Thumbnail surrogate for those six documents reduced to outdoor building shots.

video. Without user context, the automated process has no guidance on what to extract, but through emphasis on particular named entity associations, these skims can be produced. Figure 4.6 also hints at the multimedia collage possibilities from multiple views: the Shot Thumbnails storyboard when filtered to outdoor building shots shows a visual surrogate of the scenery within the selected six video documents.

The type of video skim represented in Figure 4.6 is a form of semantic compression, regulating the contents of the multimedia presentation based on personal interests. Traditional compression involves eliminating redundancies, such as through entropy encoding as is used with the popular *zip* compression. Source encoding can also be used that acknowledges human perception limitations and removes data inperceptible to people, as is used with mp3 compression for audio.

Armed with more context of personal interest, however, further compression is possible. Examples include keeping face shots and emphasizing face regions with greater resolution than surrounding areas, and removing video segments where no speech is detected. Exploration of such rules has been done for the TRECVID Video Summarization task [88], but the context has been too weak for the BBC Rushes to offer performance advantages over the fast-forward technique. Leveraging from human manipulation with interactive surrogates, as in selecting entities and entity types, does provide strong context for the dynamic extraction of material for a playable tailored video skim.

4.3   REFLECTIONS/EXERCISES

1. Design an audio-only multimedia surrogate. What advantages does it offer? What are the disadvantages?

2. How do you decide whether a multimedia surrogate has value? How in text retrieval has value been ascribed to document surrogates such as titles, abstracts, etc.?

3. Consider the illustrated views of Informedia for video collections in the figures: Shot Thumbnails, Timelines, VIBE, etc. How would these views alter the typical online video collection experience today, e.g., with YouTube or an online news source.

· · · ·

CHAPTER 5

End-User Utility for Metadata and Surrogates: Effectiveness, Efficiency, and Satisfaction

Up to this point, the lecture has presented automated descriptive metadata and its use in various surrogates without emphasizing the utility, i.e., usability, of those surrogates and search capabilities against the metadata: do they matter, and are they any good? Usability is defined in an international standard (ISO 9241) as the extent to which a computer system or product enables users to achieve specified goals in a given context of use efficiently and effectively while promoting feelings of satisfaction. These three metrics of efficiency, effectiveness, and satisfaction appear throughout the human–computer interaction (HCI) literature. Efficiency addresses whether one can finish the task in reasonable time. Effectiveness deals with whether one can produce a quality solution. Satisfaction considers whether one would be willing or eager to repeat the experience again. The three metrics may be correlated, e.g., a surrogate that is very satisfying may motivate its user to greater performance and hence higher effectiveness, whereas conversely an unsatisfying interface may produce extremely slow activity leading to poor efficiency. These three usability aspects are discussed elsewhere in greater detail as they relate to HCI research in general, with the conclusion that all three are necessary to obtain an accurate assessment of an interface's usability [97].

Context also matters in assessing utility: who are the users and what are their tasks? Foraker Design defines ecological validity as follows [98]:

> Ecological validity—the extent to which the context of a user study matches the context of actual use of a system, such that it is reasonable to suppose that the results of the study are representative of actual usage and that the differences in context are unlikely to impact the conclusions drawn. All factors of how the study is constructed must be considered: how representative are the tasks, the users, the context, and the computer systems?

Ecological validity is often difficult for multimedia information retrieval researchers for a number of reasons. The data in hand may not be representative, e.g., the use of the Corel professional image database will not be represent amateur collections such as the average individual's digital photograph collection. The tasks used may be artificial, e.g., finding a factual date from a news video corpus may be a task that in practice is always achieved through a newspaper text archive rather than a broadcast news archive. The users may not represent actual users, with university research often substituting college students as the user study subjects because of their availability. Finally, the context is likely different between the user study and an actual work environment, with an actual work environment having time and accuracy pressures that are difficult to simulate in a short-term study. A few Informedia user studies will be reviewed in light of these definitions, moving to TREC Video Retrieval Evaluation (TRECVID) as a community supporting open metrics-based evulations. A discussion of exploratory search concludes this section, a task type not yet covered well in multimedia surrogate evaluations.

5.1   INFORMEDIA EXPERIMENTS ON VARIOUS VIDEO SURROGATES

The utility and efficiency of the layout and content of Informedia surrogates illustrated in prior figures, including Figures 4.2 and 4.3, are reported in detail elsewhere [81, 99, 100, 93], validated through a number of usability methods, including transaction log analysis, contextual inquiry, heuristic evaluation, and cognitive walkthroughs. Formal studies allow facets of surrogate interfaces to be compared for statistically significant differences in dependent measures such as success rate and time on task. An early Informedia formal empirical study was conducted to determine the relative merits of a single thumbnail to represent video documents, comparing a Segment Grid menu of document thumbnails and scores versus a text menu of document titles and scores [78]. Figure 5.1 shows examples of the three tested interfaces in a within-subjects design.

Thirty high school and college students participated in an experiment using a fact-finding task against a documentary video corpus, where dependent measures included correctness, time to

FIGURE 5.1: Three interface treatments for a set of video documents in user study [78]: text view (left), using the first shot thumbnail for each document, and using the query-based shot thumbnail (right) for each document.

complete the task, and subjective satisfaction. The study had high ecological validity because such students typically are shown documentaries and later asked to recall presented facts or produce reports based on the information within the documentaries. As such, questions on who would benefit and why from this study are easily answered: high school and college students would benefit, because finding material from documentary videos could be made more effective, efficient, and satisfying. The study found that when the thumbnail image is chosen based on the query context, users complete the task more quickly and with greater satisfaction with such an interface than when using plain text menus containing no imagery, or when using a context-independent thumbnail menu, in which each document is always represented by the same thumbnail selection strategy of taking the first shot in the document. A simple thumbnail selection strategy did not distinguish itself from a straight text presentation. However, if the thumbnail to represent a video document is chosen based on where the query terms appear with the greatest score (a combination of density of matches and importance of matches as returned by the text search, image search, map search, or whatever search engine was used), then that query-based thumbnail does produce faster, more accurate, more satisfying retrieval performance. This result, in which surrogates chosen based on context produce a more efficient interface, was discussed in a previous chapter regarding temporal video skims and is a frequent conclusion of Informedia studies.

Informedia storyboards, shown as a surrogate for a single video document in Figure 3.4 and for a set of documents in Figure 3.9, were evaluated primarily through discount usability techniques, two of which were heuristic evaluation and think-aloud protocol. Heuristic evaluation is a usability engineering method for finding the usability problems in a user interface design so that they can be attended to as part of an iterative design process [101]. Heuristic evaluation involves having a set of evaluators independently examine the interface and judge its compliance with recognized usability principles (the "heuristics"). The findings are aggregated, producing a prioritized list of usability problems in the interface with references to principles that were violated by the design in each case in the opinion of the evaluator [102]. With the think-aloud protocol, a small set of users are asked to describe the contents of their working memory while they perform video retrieval tasks with someone observing them and taking notes. By listening to users think aloud while performing tasks, one can infer their line of thought, what they expected from the system, what problems they faced, and their reactions. Pioneering work with think-aloud protocol shows it to be an effective "discount" usability engineering method, capable of uncovering errors at cost savings after trials with only a few users. Its primary disadvantage is that requiring the user to reflect on and vocalize the interactions with the system introduces added burden on the user, which would not be there in actual system use. The observer plays an interruptive role, the users face increased strain and cognitive load, and users may not vocalize when the task becomes difficult. As a result, the think-aloud technique is typically used along with other usability engineering methods to compensate for its deficiencies [103]. The use of these techniques for storyboard evaluation has been published in the context of TRECVID tasks [80].

Storyboards were found to be an ideal road map into a video possessing a number of shots, e.g., the user can quickly navigate to the video represented in Figure 3.4 by clicking on a thumbnail in the storyboard that provides a visual table of contents, rather than linearly playing the video to that point. Of course, for some video like long sequences of a single person talking as seen in the HistoryMakers collection, the whole video is a single shot of that person's head, and a storyboard of that one shot provides no navigational value. When there is a multiplicity of shots, storyboards can be very effective.

As for ecological validity, in practice Informedia users were struggling more with the task of finding the right shot from a collection of videos, rather than just finding the right shot within a single video, once the corpus grew from tens to hundreds to thousands of hours. The obvious interface extension for presentations such as those shown Figure 3.4 was to present all of the shots for a set of video segments, e.g., all of the shots for the 354 segments shown in part in Figure 3.9. Such a multiple document storyboard would directly address the actual user's task of finding the right shot from a collection of video, but the interface characteristics change. If all the shots for the 354 segments are shown, the storyboard would contain 10,054 shots, a much greater number of thumbnails than is likely to be efficiently scanned by the storyboard interface. Hence, a major difficulty with storyboards serving as multimedia collection surrogates is that there are often too many shots to display in a single screen. The lesson of the thumbnail-query context study applies to this situation: the user's query context can indicate which shots to emphasize in an abbreviated display. Rather than show all the shots, only those shots containing matches (i.e., 1204 shots, rather than 10,054 for Figure 3.9) can be included in a representation for a collection of video.

Other Informedia published empirical studies include the following:

- Benefits of text accompanying storyboard thumbnails, if interleaved and reduced from a full transcript [85], the study overviewed earlier with Figure 4.1.
- Benefits of video skims whose audio is broken at natural silence boundaries with phrases emphasized over words and kept synchronized to visuals [1].
- Utility of multimedia collages emphasizing named entities and visuals emphasizing faces [96].
- Dependence, even overdependence, of college students on text search when using a video retrieval system [104].
- Interface redesign that successfully promoted within college student users other search types in addition to text, namely, querying with an image and querying for a visual concept such as "buildings" [105].

A community effort to assemble test sets, produce ground truth, establish metrics, and communicate tasks representing real world use helps to advance multimedia retrieval research, so that work in setting up studies such as the cited Informedia list does not need to be done from scratch for each research team, to better replicate and extend each other's work, and to do so in an open framework. The next section discusses how TRECVID was formed to fulfill this role.

5.2   NIST TRECVID ON FACT-FINDING SHOT-BASED RETRIEVAL

The National Institute of Standards and Technology (NIST) TREC was started in 1992 to support the text retrieval industry by providing the infrastructure necessary for large-scale evaluation of text retrieval methodologies. At that time, the Cranfield tradition of using retrieval experiments on test collections was already well established, but progress in the text information retrieval field was hampered by the lack of easily accessible, realistically large test collections. Large test collections did exist, but they were proprietary, with each collection usually the result of a single company's efforts. The proprietary nature of the collections also biased them in various ways. TREC was conceived as a way to address this need for large, unbiased test collections.

The same needs for the video retrieval community led to the establishment of the TREC Video Track in 2001. Now an independent evaluation, TRECVID began with the goal of promoting progress in content-based retrieval from digital video via open, metrics-based evaluation. The corpora have ranged from documentaries to advertising films to broadcast news, and benchmark tasks include shot detection, visual feature detection, and interactive search as overviewed by Smeaton et al. [33]. The corpus has grown from early years to be more representative of large video information sets. The TRECVID 2004 test set was 128 broadcasts, about 70 hours, of ABC News and CNN Headline News video from 1998, consisting of 33,367 reference shots. The TRECVID 2005 test set was 85 hours (140 international broadcasts) of English, Arabic, and Chinese news from 2004, consisting of 45,765 reference shots. TRECVID 2006 is similar to TRECVID 2005 but with more data: 165 hours of U.S., Arabic, and Chinese news with 79,484 common reference shots. TRECVID 2007 and 2008 switches from broadcast news to Dutch television materials as detailed in the TRECVID online proceedings [58].

The Cranfield paradigm of retrieval evaluation is based on a test collection consisting of three components: a set of documents, a set of information need statements called topics, and a set of relevance judgments. The relevance judgments are a list of the "correct answers" to the searches: the documents that should be retrieved for each topic. Success is measured based on quantities of relevant documents retrieved, in particular, the metrics of recall and precision. The two are combined into a single measure of performance, average precision, which measures precision after each relevant document is retrieved for a given topic. Average precision is then itself averaged over all of the topics to produce a mean average precision (MAP) metric for evaluating a system's performance.

For TRECVID video searches, the individual "documents" retrieved are shots, where a shot is defined as a single continuous camera operation without an editor's cut, fade, or dissolve—typically 2–10 seconds long for broadcast news. The TRECVID search task is defined as follows: given a multimedia statement of information need (a topic) and the common shot reference, return a ranked list of up to 1000 shots from the reference that best satisfy the need. For interactive search, the interactive user has no previous knowledge of the search test collection or topics. With this task, the usability ISO 9241 definition becomes: the extent to which a video retrieval system enables users to identify relevant shots from news video efficiently and effectively while promoting feelings of satisfaction.

To address ecological validity, the topics are defined by NIST to reflect many of the types of queries real users pose, based on query logs against video corpora such as the BBC Archives and other empirical data [33, 106]. The topics include requests for specific items or people and general instances of locations and events, reflecting the Panofsky–Shatford mode/facet matrix of specific, generic, and abstract subjects of pictures [14].

User studies conducted with TRECVID topics on TRECVID data can make use of the TRECVID community effort to claim ecological validity in most regards: the data set is real and representative, the tasks (topics) are representative based on previous analysis of BBC and other empirical data, and the processing efforts are well communicated with a set of rules for all to follow. The remaining question of validity is whether the subject pool represents a broader set of users, with university students and staff for the most part comprising the subject pool for many research groups because of their availability. Over the years, Informedia TRECVID experiments have confirmed the utility of storyboards showing matching thumbnails across multiple video documents [80], the differences in expert and novice search behavior when given TRECVID topics [105], the utility of transcript text for news video topics [34], and the neglected use of feature filters (e.g., include or exclude all shots having the "roads" feature or "outdoors" feature) to reduce the shot space [34, 80, 104].

One important lesson from the TRECVID research community in general has been the dominating performance on search tasks when a human is in the loop. Automated tool support in combination with human manipulation and interpretation offer tremendous leverage in addressing the challenge of video information retrieval. Without automated tools, the human user is swamped with too many possibilities as the quantity and diversity of video accessible on the Web proliferate. Ignoring the human user, though, is a mistake. Fully automated systems involving no human user have consistently and significantly underperformed compared to interactive human-in-the-loop search systems evaluated in the video search tasks of the NIST TREC Video Retrieval evaluation forum (TRECVID); see Christel and Yan [10] for further discussion and NIST [58] for reports on past work.

Another lesson from TRECVID is the benefit of multiple modes of querying into the video set, i.e., selecting subsets of video documents based on their metadata. Today's commercial video search engines often rely on filename and accompanying text sources [60]. Users issue text queries to retrieve nonlinguistic visual imagery. The image retrieval community has focused on content-based indexed by pixel-level image attributes such as color, texture, and shape [6, 60], where users supply a visual example as the search key, but the underlying low-level attributes makes it difficult for the user to formulate queries. In an attempt at bridging this semantic gap, the multimedia research community has invested in developing a Large-Scale Concept Ontology for Multimedia, whereby semantic visual features such as "road" or "people" can be used for video retrieval [59]. These three access strategies—query-by-text, query-by-image example, and query-by-concept—can be used to produce storyboard surrogates matching the issued query. In the past 5 years, interactive retrieval systems evaluated in TRECVID have almost universally supported query-by-text, with that functionality responsible for most of the information retrieval success through TRECVID 2004 [34]. Query-by-image example is the next most frequently supported strategy across TRECVID participants [34, 58, 107], with query-by-concept not having success in early 2003–2004 trials [53, 108] and not being implemented and tested as widely as the other query strategies.

All three strategies (query by text, image, concept) have been used to produce storyboard layouts of imagery by the Carnegie Mellon Informedia video search engine [10, 80, 104, 105] and the MediaMill video search engine [9, 60] for a number of years, with these systems scoring best for all of the TRECVID interactive video search evaluations in which they participated: 2002, 2003, 2004, 2005, and 2006. Hence, there is evidence that the three query strategies together are effective for the TRECVID search tasks, but there is a qualification. Those top-scoring runs have consistently been produced by "expert" runs, as discussed by Christel and Yan [10], rather than novices.

TRECVID as an evaluation forum does have its shortcomings. Automated tools, when presented poorly, can lead to frustration or be ignored, but this is not often caught by TRECVID interactive search task reports. TRECVID interactive evaluations historically have emphasized only information retrieval effectiveness measures (e.g., MAP), and not other measures (e.g., satisfaction, efficiency) of end user utility. The vast majority of TRECVID interactive runs have been conducted by the researchers themselves posing as users [58], with a few notable exceptions [53, 80, 104, 108, 105]. Even these exceptions, though, use students as subjects rather than real-world users. The Informedia surrogates and TRECVID tasks were studied with a small set of real-world users mining open source data sets: government intelligence analysts, reported on in detail by Christel [109], with a few reflections on that work repeated here.

Regarding the interfaces, when attributes of a target user community are known, such as the text search expertise of intelligence analysts, the interface should be tuned to work as a better tool leveraging from that expertise and user expectations. For example, the analysts all assumed the existence of a state-of-the-art text search interface, so when basic functionality such as spelling correction was not provided, they were confused and annoyed. The Informedia storyboard surrogate (Figure 3.9) succeeded in communicating thousands of shots per 15-minute search topic to the analysts. Its efficiency traces back to recommendations from Christel and Moraveji [80] based on the work of Shneiderman et al. [110] to "capture user interaction history," "provide consistent features," "enable informed choices," and "facilitate efficient investigations."

As noted above, the three query strategies (by text, image, and concept) together are effective for the TRECVID search tasks in the hands of experts. The expert runs establish idealistic upper bounds on performance, at the expense of assuming certain knowledge and motivation by the expert users. The term "expert" refers to a user with three sources of knowledge not possessed by "novices": (1) the expert has been working with multimedia information retrieval research for at least a year, having a better sense of the accuracy of various automated video processing techniques; (2) the expert has used the tested video retrieval system before the timed runs with the TRECVID data, perhaps even contributing to its development, and therefore knows the system operation better than study participants who first see it during the test run; and (3) the expert knows about TRECVID evaluation, e.g., the emphasis on shot-based retrieval and use of MAP as a key metric. Both experts and novices are ignorant of the search topics and the test collection contents, in accordance with the Cranfield paradigm and TRECVID interactive search task. The focus of Christel's study [109] is understanding the utility of query-by-image and query-by-concept for novices, the intelligence analysts who have worked with text sources of data and have no implicit motivation to score well according to standard TRECVID metrics and are using the given video surrogates for the first time. A within-subjects study found that analysts strongly prefer to have all three means of querying rather than a system with just query-by-text, and that the full system with all three query capabilities is easier to learn and easier to use. The analysts perform significantly better with such a complete system versus having only a text query capability. The result is interesting in that these analysts were very proficient in text search systems and strategies (and hence one might have expected a bias toward query-by-text).

Regarding TRECVID and ecological validity, the subject pools should be people outside of the system research and development group, i.e., "novices" instead of "experts" using our parlance, because past studies [104, 105, 109] confirm that novices and experts will use the system differently. Ideally, representatives of the target community can participate, as was done with the analysts. Work with analysts showed that sports topics carry no meaning for this group, and that the metric of MAP at a depth of 1000 shots is also unrealistic (the analysts figured that collecting tens of relevant shots were enough to satisfy the search task, rather than hundreds or a thousand).

The value of a common TRECVID benchmark for evaluation helps considerably, but of course "video search" is much broader than the shot-based retrieval from video corpora discussed here. Analyst activity is creative and exploratory as well, where the information need is discovered and evolves over time based on interplay with data sources. Likewise, video search activity can be creative and exploratory where the information need is discovered and evolves over time. The next section discusses exploratory search and one study with HistoryMakers data looking into differences between fact-finding and exploratory tasks.

5.3   EXPLORATORY USE OF MULTIMEDIA INFORMATION SYSTEMS

An exploratory search "may be characterized by the presence of some search technology and information objects that are inherently meaningful to users...often motivated by a complex information problem, and a poor understanding of terminology and information space structure" [111]. Marchionini breaks down three types of search activities—lookup, learn, and investigate—noting exploratory search as especially pertinent to the learn and investigate activities [112]. TRECVID interactive search studies with users given a stated topic, are solely in the "lookup" category, as are the tasks in many traditional information retrieval forums studying fact retrieval or question answering. Using the HistoryMakers corpus, a study was conducted requiring learning and investigating activities [113], which Marchionini further breaks down as follows [112]:

- Learn: knowledge acquisition, comprehension, interpretation, comparison, aggregation/integration, socialization
- Investigate: accretion, analysis, exclusion/negation, synthesis, evaluation, discovery, planning/forecasting, transformation

Not surprisingly, the teaching professionals at a summer 2007 workshop for HistoryMakers beta testing [113] were quite interested in the use of the HistoryMakers Digital Library for more than just traditional fact retrieval and lookup, but also for these learning and investigating activities. Hence, two studies were conducted in autumn 2007: one with a treasure hunt lookup task, and the other with an exploratory task [113]. The studies investigated the role of motion video in the interfaces: HistoryMakers stories are presented in one of two ways in two within-subjects experiments: either as audio accompanied by a single still photographic image per story (still), or as the same audio within a motion video of the interviewee speaking (video), as illustrated in Figure 5.2.

For treasure hunt lookup, significantly more text searches were issued in the 20-minute sessions than with exploratory search, regardless of interface treatment. With exploratory search, significantly more time is spent playing stories regardless of format (still or video) versus the treasure hunt task. In the lookup task, subjects were driven to find facts, being ignorant of the oral history visual presentation differences. Subjects showed no significant preference for either the still or video

FIGURE 5.2: Story playback window: in studies [113], story is either video or a still image (same audio for both).

treatment, and no difference in task performance. For exploratory search, video presentation had a significant positive effect on user satisfaction [113].

A previous eye-tracking empirical study looked at digital video surrogates composed of text and three thumbnail images to represent each document, and found that participants looked at and fixated on text far more than pictures [84]. They used the text as an anchor from which to make judgments about the list of results. The authors conclude that perhaps the task may have affected performance, but no evidence for such an influence was found [84]. In the pair of HistoryMakers studies [113], we do have a body of evidence suggesting different foci of interest within the story playback interface of Figure 5.2.

For fact lookup, subjects focused on the lower half of the interface, the text transcript, whereas for the exploratory task, they acknowledged and expressed a strong preference for the upper half being motion video. Given a targeted search task, text representation dominates user attention. For exploratory search tasks, participants learning and investigating through a greater frequency of story playback express a strong preference for motion video representations of the oral history interviews.

For the first impressions study [113], the 20-minute time limit was restrictive, especially for the exploratory task. So that users would not be overwhelmed with interface choices, text search was emphasized; however, the resulting subjective scores are low, with the low-rated satisfaction supplemented by open-ended text comments asking for more ways to browse the oral histories and more access strategies than just text search. In fact, prior portions of this lecture discuss and present other Informedia surrogates offering many additional exploratory interfaces such as map and time-line views and VIBE plots. As noted in the paper [113], these two studies were conducted with a streamlined interface to focus on the "still" versus "video" question for first-time users of the corpus, but even the short-term study here suggests that for exploratory search, users want more options. They made use of image search for 5% of their issued searches, for example, as opposed to image search being used for only 0.5% of the searches in the treasure hunt task.

Marchionini [112] notes that searches supporting investigation involve multiple iterations that may take place over long periods. Shneiderman and Plaisant [114] acknowledge that evaluating tools for exploratory, creative work is difficult, and call out the need for longitudinal research with multidimensional in-depth long-term case studies (MILC). Ideally, MILC research could be conducted with the campuses, faculty, and students involved in The HistoryMakers testing, i.e., those participants from the Summer 2007 Workshop, to see changing patterns of use and utility as the faculty and students gain familiarity and experience with the system. Such research is a logical extension to the reported "first impressions" research [113]. In the term "multidimensional in-depth long-term case studies" the *multidimensional* aspect refers to using observations, interviews, surveys, as well as automated logging to assess user performance and interface efficacy and utility. The *in-depth* aspect is the intense engagement of the researchers with the real users to the point of becoming a partner or assistant. *Long-term* refers to longitudinal studies that begin with training in use of a specific tool through proficient usage that leads to strategy changes for the expert users. *Case studies* refer to the detailed reporting about a small number of individuals working on their own problems, in their normal environment.

The conclusion that for fact-finding lookup search tasks, text representation dominates user attention [113] has been seen as well in the logs of user interaction data from numerous universities' history and African American Studies students in 2007 and 2008 accessing the HistoryMakers Digital Library. These students make use of the Common Text view (Figure 3.6) almost exclusively as opposed to the other available surrogates. The same pattern of use was found with six intelligence analysts given stated information topics (from TRECVID tasks): the Common Text view, along with text titling for video segments, text transcripts, and text search, were heavily accessed [93, 109]. First-time system users accessing either oral history or news video began with and stayed primarily with text-based representations [93]. This use argues for textual representation of descriptive metadata for multimedia repositories, and indexing and interfaces promoting the efficient use of such text.

As to the value of other forms of medata, in a first hour with the Informedia system these additional means are not utilized, perhaps because of inherent deficiencies but also very likely due to their being different from more traditional "issue text search, get ranked list of results" information lookup interactions. Only by working with a set of users over time might these additional views get noticed and used in exploratory tasks, with quantitative usage data and qualitative feedback offering insights into their true utility.

Evaluating the benefits of other types of metadata and interfaces for exploratory search needs to incorporate MILC, especially the longitudinal aspect. First-time users such as the analysts accessing Informedia as reported by Christel [109] and [93] stayed with text-based sources even for exploratory search. True end users of video collections—not the video indexing researchers themselves, but the end user community—often have poor understanding of what dimensions are available for searching and exploring in a video collection (e.g., face detection seems to work, so vehicle detection should work just as well, or specific face recognition). Automatic speech recognition produces fine transcripts of talk in the studio, so it should work just as well for field reporting. Of course, there are many pitfalls to automated multimedia content-based indexing and such end user assumptions often result in disappointment. A challenge in building search interfaces and multimedia surrogates is to account for variability in the correctness of the underlying metadata and let the user explore through it, e.g., deciding whether to increase precision by dropping out low-confidence automated measures or increase recall by including them.

Gersh et al. [115] discuss how exploring a set of information can help an analyst synthesize, understand, and present a coherent explanation of what it tells us about the world. Marchionini and Geisler [112, 116] discuss agile views of files in the Open Video Digital Library: overviews of collections of video segments and previews of specific video objects, supporting Shneiderman's Information Seeking Mantra with dynamic interactive querying. The Informedia research group has emphasized a multiplicity of views for information seeking, encouraging exploration, and providing insight from interactions with a large video corpus, but evaluation with respect to MILC and exploratory search is still lacking in part due to the lack of open benchmark community support (as in TRECVID) for such work. TRECVID may very well broaden its scope to cover other issues in video search besides fact-finding, e.g., the exploratory discovery of materials in video corpora rather than seeking relevant materials for a known, expressed need. The assessment strategies should broaden as well, embracing the use of MILC. Ideally, MILC research could be conducted with representatives of a real user community over time, to see changing patterns of use and utility as the users gain familiarity and experience with the system. An open question is how far multimedia information systems researchers can go in measuring the utility of their tools by the success achieved by the users they are studying, i.e., a way to keep technical developments in synergy with human needs.

In general, there are three significant hurdles that should be addressed in evaluating interactive, exploratory interfaces for multimedia information: (1) corpus size; (2) task definition; and (3) time with the users. Users want and need a large corpus to explore. The nature of exploratory search is that users will rummage through peripheral material, discover some aspect of interest in a tangent, and in that tangent go probing for additional material without running into the boundaries of the test corpus. If the corpus is not large enough, there will not be a rich enough periphery for any new discoveries, and there will not be enough material to support various tangential directions of inquiry. Users want to explore their own topic, not someone else's stated topic. The very nature of stating the topic already moves it toward more directed search. Users will start simple and with what they know from previous experience. The most important challenge for evaluating exploratory multimedia information systems is to conduct long-term investigations, the "L" from the MILC framework. As users' search strategies mature and their comfort levels and expertise with a system increase, the utility of other features such as the many views overviewed in the section on surrogates for collection understanding can be truly assessed. Examples with respect to these three hurdles are detailed in [93] from two test Informedia user communities: students working with the HistoryMakers, and analysts working with broadcast news.

5.4   REFLECTIONS/EXERCISES

1. Define a few scenarios of a user community, type of multimedia information set, and collection of tasks. For your scenario, argue for the relative importance of effectiveness, efficiency, and satisfaction. Are they equally weighted?

2. Select an online video site and formulate a few fact-finding and exploratory topics suited to that site's materials (see [113] for examples of these two types of topics). Discuss the utility of the site's interfaces for the two topic types.

3. Look to the CIVR Video Olympics for 2007 and 2008 (using TRECVID 2006 and 2007 data, respectively), or watch the video for "VideOlympics 2007" at http://www.youtube.com/

watch?v=-QmhEguCoZ0. What type of surrogates do you see for shot-based TRECVID retrieval? What features are typical across the shown systems? What unique features, either that you saw or by your own design, would you add in to better achieve these stated fact-finding tasks?

4. Look to the field of visual analytics: enabling users to overcome information overload so that they can detect the expected and discover the unexpected through visual interfaces [117]. Consider how this research area applies to the various presented surrogates and metadata types, and to the evaluation of exploratory search against multimedia corpora. Select a portion of the online book on the topic [118] and discuss in relation to multimedia information exploration.

. . . .

CHAPTER 6

Conclusions

This lecture began with definitions and then an overview of automated descriptive metadata techniques. User involvement can improve the metadata through:

- User correction: Automatic techniques will produce errors, but have review and edit tools to allow for easy correction, e.g., marking those shots in a storyboard supposedly of only automobiles that do not contain automobiles.
- User control: Include confidence attributes in metadata so that the user can filter to only high confidence multimedia objects or consider even low confidence items, controlling the trade-off between precision and recall.
- User context: Improve accuracy of automated processing through knowledge of the multimedia genre and user tasks with it, e.g., folding in specific, relevant sources of knowledge for automatic speech recognition (ASR) and named entities, and incorporating rules on text sizes and placement for video optical character recognition (VOCR).

Other strategies for improving metadata descriptor accuracy include more computation-intensive algorithms such as optical flow, and taking advantage of temporal redundancy in multimedia information. Multimedia surrogates representing a single multimedia document or sets of documents also can be improved through interactive user control and user context. For example, the fast-forward surrogate of playing a BBC rushes source video at 50× to produce a 2% summary leverages no context aside from the removal of "junk" frames (color bars, scene clappers) [92]. Users interacting with a surrogate such as a named entity tree identify what document set and which entity pairs they care about within the set, allowing for very tailored but very playable video skim summaries to be produced, as shown in Figure 4.6. User context improves the utility of multimedia surrogates. As another example, the user's query context can easily produce a set of hundreds of multimedia documents with 10,000 shots in even a small corpus such as the TREC Video Retrieval Evaluation (TRECVID) 2006 test set. Through query context, a storyboard can show just the 1000 shots temporally related to the query match terms rather than the full set of 10,000, with user control allowing further drill-down of the storyboard shot set to just those with attributes such as faces and buildings.

TRECVID as an evaluation forum has let the multimedia information retrieval community chart progress in shot detection (a consistent success—90% or higher accuracy), visual feature classification (varied success, with features such as faces easy but others such as weapons quite difficult), and interactive search. For the shot-based directed search information retrieval task evaluated at TRECVID, storyboards have consistently and overwhelmingly produced the best performance. Motivated users can navigate through thousands of shot thumbnails in storyboards, better even than with an "extreme video retrieval" interface based on rapid serial visual presentation of keyframes [10, 119]. For TRECVID 2006 topics, users could on average see and judge 2487 shots per 15-minute topic [10]. The storyboard provides a packed visual overview with trivial interactive control needed for zooming, filtering, and getting to full multimedia document detail, in accordance with Shneiderman's Visual Information-Seeking Mantra: "overview, zoom and filter, details on demand" [120].

Storyboards are not sufficient as the only multimedia surrogate of value, however. One weakness is with visually homogenous results, e.g., results from a color search perhaps, or a corpus of just lecture slides, or just head-and-shoulder shots where shots in the storyboard are not visually distinctive from one another. There also are many more tasks to accomplish with a multimedia corpus than just shot-based fact-finding as studied with TRECVID interactive search. Storyboards fail to show overviews of other metadata information facets such as time, space, and named entities. Answering tasks such as when or where disasters occurred, who was involved with baseball in the 1940s, etc., bring in the need for other surrogates as reviewed in this paper. Multiple, cooperating views allow for greater collection understanding, a holistic view of the contents of hundreds of multimedia documents with thousands of shots. Finally, a set of surrogates or agile views allows for various types of search activities to be pursued. Storyboards are quite effective for lookup (fact-finding, i.e., solving a stated or understood need). A suite of surrogates, building from a suite of aural, visual, and textual metadata, can also address learning and investigating activities. These exploratory search activities advance the user from finding to understanding [112].

Historically, information retrieval forums such as TREC and then TRECVID and computer science venues such as the Association for Computing Machinery Special Interest Group on Information Retrieval (ACMSIGIR) have emphasized lookup tasks. Exploratory search and encouraging understanding from interactions with multimedia information systems is admittedly a primary goal of university educators and lifelong learners. In particular, for The HistoryMakers video life oral histories, humanities professors were quite eager to encourage exploratory search in their students and emphasized learning and investigating over lookup tasks [113].

Evaluating exploratory search in multimedia information retrieval remains a challenge. The "Multi-dimensional In-depth Long-term Case studies" strategy was offered as a roadmap for such evaluation. The information visualization field, and in particular the field of visual analytics, have increased attention to the problems but also the importance of evaluation in recent years, and a number of publications are slated (e.g., *IEEE Computer Graphics and Applications* special issue on Visual Analytics Evaluation for 2009) that will offer insights. Visual analytics is the science of analytical reasoning facilitated by interactive visual interfaces. Whereas many researchers in visual analytics are working with primarily text information sets, this work naturally will address multimedia information systems to a greater degree as significantly large benchmark test sets of multimedia become established.

There are numerous other future opportunities for automated or semiautomated metadata generation for multimedia information systems. Social networking and tagging have proven as extremely viable in e-commerce and online communities such as Flickr and YouTube. The sheer volume of contributions allows for success, at least in terms of precision, even if only a small fraction of contributors ever tag their materials. For example, in an October 2008 talk, a Google manager noted that 13 hours of video are uploaded every minute of every day to YouTube. For almost any lookup task, there is a good chance that a contributor at some point tagged their video with terms allowing for a match. Viewers can also add tag data and recommendations for most online video properties, and for many their search and viewing activities are tracked to serve as another form of metadata so that a viewer with a similar profile in the future could be provided with tailored recommendations. A press release from comScore notes that in July 2008 Americans viewed more than 11.4 billion online videos for a total of 558 million hours during the month. The increasing activity of online viewing and online publication merits attention, but is beyond the scope of this lecture. A lesson that hopefully has been gleaned from this lecture, though, is the value of multiple descriptors, both in terms of modality (aural, visual, and textual), and in terms of the syntax-semantics pyramid conceptual framework for classifying visual content [19]. Contributor-added tags may be shallow. For temporal multimedia documents, metadata from social networking and tagging is anticipated to be very shallow because not even the most dedicated users will have the stamina to classify ever-growing content as it changes visually and aurally through a presentation. It is the temporal component of multimedia, its tedium, and cost to review and annotate, that keep it likely that automated processing will maintain a role in descriptive metadata generation for the future. Google itself has an audioindexing ASR effort "GAUDI" within their research laboratories, acknowledging that such automated indexing not only allows multimedia documents to be located, but also allows users to locate the region of interest within that document [121]. A major benefit of automated techniques such as ASR, VOCR, named entity tagging from spoken narrative, visual feature classification of shots, etc., is that these are all temporally aligned to the source multimedia object.

A few other trends worth mentioning from both the online video communities and research forums such as ACM Multimedia is the recognition that amateurs are eager to be not only consumers but also producers of multimedia content, and that "multimedia information" is increasingly being used not only for communication but also for entertainment or as an art form. This lecture emphasized TRECVID 2006 and the HistoryMakers in its examples, both professionally produced sets of video emphasizing communication. Automatic production of metadata and surrogates that build from such descriptors will likely have much different characteristics when targeting amateur video meant for a variety of purposes. For example, knowledge sources for ASR could be tailored for personal interests, and visual feature classification built from training sets typical of hand-held amateur video with degradation in camera shake, framing, and lighting.

With respect to visual, aural, and text modalities, we can do text information retrieval relatively well and thus far have defaulted multimedia information retrieval (IR) to make use of text IR wherever possible. Visual and aural automated processing techniques are difficult and hence researchers often begin with tuned test data sets where results do not generalize. Some notable exceptions include face detection, which has worked well across different corpora. By capturing more and better metadata at creation time, using folksonomies and aggregated usage statistics, developing intermediate semantic concepts through Large-Scale Concept Ontology for Multimedia efforts, and rewarding research working with representative benchmark sets, we can slowly migrate multimedia IR toward better performance levels enjoyed by text retrieval. Given the difficulty of automating multimedia IR for general corpora, the role of the human user to guide and filter retrieval should be optimized. Continuing research with multimedia information systems will look to leverage the intelligence and goals of human users in accessing multimedia contents meeting their needs, rather than overwhelming them with exponentially expanding amounts of irrelevant materials. Directions include applying lessons from the human–computer interaction and information visualization fields and being pulled by user-driven requirements rather than just pushing technology-driven solutions.

In expanding the view of search activity from fact-finding to also exploration facilitating understanding, interactions between the user and surrogates built from metadata become even more important. Interactive fact-finding has consistently outperformed automated fact-finding in visual shot retrieval. Interactive computer vision has succeeded in delivering functionality with human intervention. Interactive use of multiple cooperating surrogates each exposing facets of the underlying multimedia information is only beginning to be investigated for exploratory search. Multimedia IR will have great impact when IR is considered not just lookup but also learning and investigating, and when it lets consumers consider growing multimedia data sets as useful assets rather than information glut.

Acknowledgment

This work is very much dependent on the contributions made by various Informedia research sponsors, partners, collaborators, and team members through the years, a record of which is kept at the Informedia web site: http://www.informedia.cs.cmu.edu. This work was supported by the National Science Foundation under Grant No. IIS-0205219 and Grant No. IIS-0705491. Special thanks to The HistoryMakers and its executive director, Julieanna Richardson, for enabling this video retrieval evaluation work with their oral history corpus. Video contributions from CNN and other sources are gratefully acknowledged for Informedia research, with thanks to NIST and the TRECVID organizers for enabling video evaluation work through the years.

References

[1] Christel, M., Smith, M., Taylor, C.R., and Winkler, D., Evolving video skims into useful multimedia abstractions, in *Proc. ACM CHI '98*, Los Angeles, CA, April, pp. 171–178 (1998). http://doi.acm.org/10.1145/274644.274670

[2] Lienhart, R., Pfeiffer, S., and Effelsberg, W., Video abstracting, *Commun. ACM*, **40**(12), 54–62 (1997). http://doi.acm.org/10.1145/265563.265572

[3] Ding, W., Marchionini, G., and Soergel, D., Multimodal surrogates for video browsing, in *Proc. ACM Conf. Digital Libraries*, Berkeley, CA, August, pp. 85–93 (1999). http://doi.acm.org/10.1145/313238.313266

[4] Jaques, R., US Surfers Flock to Web Video, Computing.co.uk (2008), www.computing.co.uk/ vnunet/news/2207678/three-quarters-surfers-watch, 21 Jan. 2008.

[5] H.J. Zhang, S.W. Smoliar, J.H. Wu, C.Y.Low, and A. Kankanhalli, A video database system for digital libraries, in *Digital Libraries: Current Issues (Digital Libraries Workshop DL '94, Newark, NJ, May 1994, Selected Papers)* (N.R. Adam, B.K. Bhargava, and Y. Yesha, Eds.), Springer, Berlin (1995).

[6] Smeulders, A.W.M., Worring, M., Santini, S., Gupta, A., and Jain, R., Content based image retrieval at the end of the early years, *IEEE Trans. PAMI*, **22**, 1349–1380 (2000). 10.1109/34.895972

[7] Markkula, M., and Sormunen, E., End-user searching challenges indexing practices in the digital newspaper photo archive, *Inf. Retrieval*, **1**(4), 259–285 (2000). 10.1023/A:1009995816485

[8] Rodden, K., Basalaj, W., Sinclair, D., and Wood, K.R., Does organization by similarity assist image browsing?, in *Proc. CHI '01*, pp. 190–197 (2001).

[9] Snoek, C., Worring, M., Koelma, D., and Smeulders, A., A learned lexicon-driven paradigm for interactive video retrieval, *IEEE Trans. Multimedia*, **9**(2), 280–292 (2007). 10.1109/TMM.2006.886275

[10] Christel, M., and Yan, R., Merging storyboard strategies and automatic retrieval for improving interactive video search, in *Proc. CIVR*, Amsterdam, July, pp. 486–493 (2007). http://doi.acm.org/10.1145/1282280.1282351

[11]   Rowe, L.A., and Jain, R., ACM SIGMM retreat report on future directions in multimedia research, *ACM Trans. Multimedia Comput. Commun. Appl.*, **1**, 3–13 (2005).

[12]   Li, G., Gupta, A., Sanocki, E., He, L., and Rui, Y., Browsing digital video, in *Proc. ACM CHI 2000*, The Hague, The Netherlands, April, pp. 169–176 (2000). http://doi.acm.org/10.1145/332040.332425

[13]   TASI (Technical Advisory Service for Images), Advice Paper: Metadata Overview (2006). Last reviewed Nov. 2006, http://www.tasi.ac.uk/advice/delivering/metadata.html.

[14]   Shatford, S., Analyzing the subject of a picture: a theoretical approach, *Cataloguing Classification Q.*, **6**(3), 39–62 (1986).

[15]   Enser, P., and Sandom, C., Towards a comprehensive survey of the semantic gap in visual image retrieval, in *Proc. Conf. Image and Video Retrieval LNCS 2728*, pp. 163–168 (2003). 10.1007/3-540-45113-7_29

[16]   Panofsky, E., *Studies in Iconology: Humanistic Themes in the Art of the Renaissance*, Oxford University Press, New York (1939).

[17]   Panofsky, E., *Meaning in the Visual Arts: Papers in and on Art History*, Doubleday Anchor Books, Garden City, NY (1955).

[18]   TASI (Technical Advisory Service for Images), Advice Paper: Challenges of Describing Images (2006). Last reviewed Nov. 2006, http://www.tasi.ac.uk/advice/delivering/pdf/metadata-challenges.pdf.

[19]   Jaimes, A., Benitez, A.B., and Jörgensen, C., Experiments for Multiple Level Classification of Visual Descriptors Contribution ISO/IEC JTC1/SC29/WG11 MPEG99/M5593, (1999) http://citeseerx.ist.psu.edu/viewdoc/summary?doi=10.1.1.41.8574.

[20]   Jaimes, A., and Chang, S.-F., A conceptual framework for indexing visual information at multiple levels, in *Proc. IS&T/SPIE Internet Imaging Conference*, SPIE vol. 3964, SPIE, Bellingham, WA, pp. 2–15 (2000).

[21]   Smith, J.R., and Chang, S.-F. An image and video search engine for the World-Wide Web, in *Proc. Storage & Retrieval for Image and Video Databases V*, San Jose, CA, February (1997).

[22]   Niblack, W., Barber, R., et al., The QBIC project: querying images by content using color, texture, and shape, in *IS&T/SPIE Storage and Retrieval for Image and Video Databases*, February (1993).

[23]   Chang, S.-F., Chen, B., and Sundaram, H., Semantic visual templates: linking visual features to semantics, in *ICIP 1998 Workshop on Content Based Video Search and Retrieval*, Chicago, IL, October (1998).

[24]   Binford, T.O., Survey of model-based image analysis systems, *Int. J. Robotics Res.* **1**(1), (Spring), 18–64 (1992). DOI: 10.1177/027836498200100103

[25] Forsyth, D.A., and Fleck, M., Body plans, in *Computer Vision and Pattern Recognition*, San Juan, Puerto Rico (1997).

[26] Pentland, A., Picard, R.W., and Sclaroff, S., Photobook: tools for content-based manipulation of image databases, in *IS&T/SPIE Storage and Retrieval for Image and Video Databases II*, pp. 37–50 (1994).

[27] Szummer, M., and Picard, R.W., Indoor-outdoor image classification, in *Proc. IEEE ICCV Workshop on Content-based Access of Image and Video Databases*, Bombay, India (1998).

[28] Vailaya, A., Jain, A., and Zhang, H.J., On image classification: city vs. landscape, in *IEEE Workshop on Content-Based Access of Image and Video Libraries*, Santa Barbara, CA, June (1998).

[29] Vailaya, A., Figueiredo, M., Jain, A., and Zhang, H.J., Content-based hierarchical classification of vacation images, in *Proc. IEEE Multimedia Systems*, Florence, Italy, June (1999).

[30] Srihari, R.K., Automatic indexing and content-based retrieval of captioned images, *IEEE Comput.*, **28**(9) (1995). 10.1109/2.410153

[31] Wactlar H., Christel M.G., et al., Lessons Learned from the creation and deployment of a terabyte digital video library, *IEEE Comp.*, **32**, 66–73 (1999). 10.1109/2.745722

[32] Yang, J., and Hauptmann, A., Annotating news video with locations, in *Proc. ACM Conf. on Image and Video Retrieval (CIVR)* (2006).

[33] Smeaton, A.F., Over, P., and Kraaij, W., Evaluation campaigns and TRECVID, in *Proc. ACM Workshop on Multimedia Information Retrieval*, Santa Barbara, CA, October, pp. 321–330 (2006).

[34] Hauptmann, A.G., and Christel, M.G., Successful approaches in the TREC Video Retrieval Evaluations, in *Proc. ACM Multimedia*, New York, October, pp. 668–675 (2004).

[35] He, X., and Deng, L., Discriminative learning for speech recognition: theory and practice, in *Synthesis Lectures on Speech and Audio Processing* (Morgan & Claypool Publishers), doi: 10.2200/S00134ED1V01Y200807SAP004 (2008).

[36] Jang, P.J., and Hauptmann, A.G., Learning to recognize speech by watching television, *IEEE Intell. Syst.*, **14**(5), 51–58 (1999). 10.1109/5254.796090

[37] Hauptmann, A.G., and Wactlar, H.D., Indexing and search of multimodal information, in *ICASSP-97 International Conf. on Acoustics, Speech and Signal Processing*, Munich, Germany, April, pp. 195–198 (1997).

[38] Witbrock, M.J., and Hauptmann, A.G., Artificial intelligence techniques in a digital video library, *J. Am. Soc. Inf. Sci.*, **49**(7), 619–632 (1998).

[39] Jones, G.J.F., Foote, J.T., Spärck Jones, K., and Young, S.J., Retrieving spoken documents by combining multiple index sources, in *Proc. SIGIR '96 Conf. on Research and Development in*

Info. Retrieval, Zurich, Switzerland, August, pp. 30–38 (1996). http://doi.acm.org/10.1145/243199.243208

[40] Witbrock, M.J., and Hauptmann, A.G., Using words and phonetic strings for efficient information retrieval from imperfectly transcribed spoken documents, in *Proc. ACM Digital Libraries Conf.*, Philadelphia, PA, July, pp. 30–35 (1997).

[41] Garofolo, J.S., Auzanne, C.G.P., and Voorhees, E.M., The TREC spoken document retrieval track: a success story, in *Proc. of the TREC Conference (TREC-8)*, Gaithersburg, MD, NIST (1999), http://trec.nist.gov/pubs/trec8/papers/trec8-sdr-overview.pdf.

[42] Shou, X.M., Sanderson, M., and Tuffs, N., The relationship of word error rate to document ranking, in *AAAI Spring Symposium Intelligent Multimedia Knowledge Management Workshop*, pp. 28–33 (2003). Available at: http://www.mind-project.org/papers/SS503XShou.pdf.

[43] Sphinx 4 Speech Recognition System, Jointly designed by Carnegie Mellon University, Sun Microsystems Laboratories, Mitsubishi Electric Research Labs, and Hewlett-Packard's Cambridge Research Lab (2008), http://www.speech.cs.cmu.edu/sphinx/twiki/bin/view/Sphinx4/WebHome, accessed Nov. 2008.

[44] SAIL, SAIL LABS Technology (2008), http://www.sail-technology.com.

[45] Xie, L., Chang, S.-F., Divakaran, A., and Sun, H., Unsupervised mining of statistical temporal structures in video, in *Video Mining*, Kluwer Academic Publishers, Boston, MA, pp. 279–307 (2003).

[46] Xu, M., Maddage, N., Xu, C.S., Kankanhalli, M., and Tian, Q., Creating audio keywords for event detection in soccer video, *Proc. IEEE Conf. Multimedia Expo*, **2**, 281–284 (2003).

[47] Xiong, Z., Radhakrishnan, R., and Divakaran, A., inventors, WO/2006/022394: Method for Identifying Highlight Segments in a Video Including a Sequence of Frames (2006), http://www.wipo.int/pctdb/en/wo.jsp?IA=JP2005015586.

[48] Xiong, Z., Zhou, X.S., Tian,Q., Rui, Y., and Huang, T.S., Semantic retrieval of video, *IEEE Signal Process. Mag.*, **23**(2), 18–27 (2006).

[49] Cai, R., Lu, L., and Hanjalic, A., Unsupervised content discovery in composite audio, in *Proc. ACM Multimedia* (Singapore, November), pp. 628–637 (2005).

[50] Enser, P.G.B., Pictorial information retrieval, *J. Document.*, **51**(2), 126–170 (2005).

[51] Rasmussen, E., Indexing images, *Annu. Rev. Inf. Sci. Technol.*, **32**, 169–196 (1997).

[52] Rodden, K., and Wood, K.R., How do people manage their digital photographs?, in *Proc. CHI*, Ft. Lauderdale, FL, April, pp. 409–416 (2003). http://doi.acm.org/10.1145/642611.642682

[53] Yang, M., Wildemuth, B., and Marchionini, G., The relative effectiveness of concept-based versus content-based video retrieval, in *Proc. ACM Multimedia*, New York, October, pp. 368–371 (2004).

[54] Chen, H.-L., and Rasmussen, E.M., Intellectual access to images, *Libr. Trends* **48**(2), 291–302 (1999).

[55] Boldareva, L., de Vries, A., and Hiemstra, D., Monitoring user-system performance in interactive retrieval tasks, in *Proc. RIAO 2004* (Avignon, France, April), pp. 474–483 (2004).

[56] Urban, J., Jose, J.M., and van Rijsbergen, C.J., An adaptive technique for content-based image retrieval, *Multimedia Tools Appl.*, **25** (2005).

[57] Naphade, M.R., and Smith, J.R., On the detection of semantic concepts at TRECVID, in *Proc. ACM Multimedia*, New York, October (2004).

[58] National Institute of Standards and Technology, *NIST TREC Video Retrieval Evaluation Online Proceedings*, 2001-current (2008), http://www-nlpir.nist.gov/projects/tvpubs/tv.pubs.org.html.

[59] Naphade, M., Smith, J.R., Tesic, J., Chang, S.-F., Hsu, W., Kennedy, L., Hauptmann, A., and Curtis, J., Large-scale concept ontology for multimedia, *IEEE Multimedia*, **13**(3), 86–91 (2006).

[60] Snoek, C., Worring, M., et al., The challenge problem for automated detection of 101 semantic concepts in multimedia, in *Proc. ACM Multimedia*, Santa Barbara, CA (2006). http://doi.acm.org/10.1145/1180639.1180727

[61] Yanagawa, A., Chang, S.-F., Kennedy, L., Hsu, W., Columbia University's Baseline Detectors for 374 LSCOM Semantic Visual Concepts, ADVENT Technical Report #222-2006-8, Columbia University, March (2007), http://www.ee.columbia.edu/~lyndon/pubs/adventtr2007-columbia374.pdf.

[62] Beitzel, S.M., Jensen, E.C., Frieder, O., Chowdhury, A., and Pass, G., Surrogate scoring for improved metasearch precision, in *Proc. ACM SIGIR '05*, pp. 583–584 (2005).

[63] Hauptmann, A., Yan, R., and Lin, W.-H., How many high-level concepts will fill the semantic gap in news video retrieval?, in *Proc. ACM Conference on Image and Video Retrieval*, Amsterdam, The Netherlands, July (2007).

[64] Chellappa, R., Roy-Chowdhury, A.K., and Zhou, S.K., Recognition of humans and their activities using video, in *Synthesis Lectures on Image, Video, and Multimedia Processing*, Morgan & Claypool Publishers, doi: 10.2200/S00002ED1V01Y200508IVM001 (2005).

[65] Sato, T., Kanade, T., Hughes, E., and Smith, M., Video OCR for digital news archive, in *Proc. IEEE Workshop on Content-Based Access of Image and Video Databases (CAIVD '98)*, Bombay, India, January, pp. 52–60 (1998).

[66] SRI International, Video Text Recognition (2008), http://www.sri.com/esd/automation/video_recog.html, accessed Oct. 2008.

[67] Schneiderman, H., and Kanade, T., Probabilistic modeling of local appearance and spatial relationships of object recognition, in *IEEE Conference on Computer Vision and Pattern Recognition*, Santa Barbara, CA, June, pp. 45–51 (1998).

[68] Pittsburgh Pattern Recognition, Recognizing and Tracking Faces and Objects (2008), http://www.pittpatt.com/, accessed Oct. 2008.

[69] Kubala, F., Schwartz, R., Stone, R., and Weischedel, R., Named entity extraction from speech, in *Proc. DARPA Workshop on Broadcast News Understanding Systems*, Lansdowne, VA, February (1998).

[70] Chen, M. -Y., Christel, M., Hauptmann, A., and Wactlar, H., Putting Active Learning into Multimedia Applications: Dynamic Definition and Refinement of Concept Classifiers, in Proc. ACM Multimedia, Singapore, November, pp. 902-911 (2005).

[71] ICV07, *IEEE Conf. on Computer Vision (ICCV) Workshop on Interactive Computer Vision (ICV 2007)*, Rio de Janeiro, Brazil, October 2007, doi: 10.1109/ICCV.2007.4408822 (2007).

[72] Lucas, B.D., and Kanade, T., An iterative image registration technique with an application to stereo vision, in *Proceedings of Imaging Understanding Workshop*, pp. 121–130 (1981).

[73] Yang, M.-H., Kriegman, D., and Ahuja, N., Detecting faces in images: a survey, *IEEE Trans. Pattern Anal. Mach. Intell. (PAMI)*, **24**(1), 34–58 (2002). 10.1109/34.982883

[74] MotionDSP, Ikena Reveal Product Overview (2008), http://www.motiondsp.com/products/IkenaReveal, accessed Oct. 2008.

[75] Satoh, S., and Kanade, T., Name-it: association of face and name in video, in *Proc. Computer Vision and Pattern Recognition*, June, 1997.

[76] Yang, J., and Hauptmann, A.G., Naming every individual in news video monologues, in *Proc. ACM Multimedia*, New York, October, pp. 580–587 (2004).

[77] Chua, T., Chang, S., Chaisorn, L., and Hsu, W., Story boundary detection in large broadcast news video archives: techniques, experience and trends, in *Proc. ACM Multimedia*, New York, pp. 656–659 (2004). http://doi.acm.org/10.1145/1027527.1027679

[78] Christel, M.G., Winkler, D.B., and Taylor, C.R., Improving access to a digital video library, in *Human-Computer Interaction INTERACT '97: IFIP TC13 International Conference on Human-Computer Interaction*, July, Sydney, Australia (S. Howard, J. Hammond, and G. Lindgaard, Eds.), Chapman & Hall, London, pp. 524–531 (1997).

[79] Christel, M., Moraveji, N., and Huang, C., Evaluating content-based filters for image and video retrieval, in *Proc. ACM SIGIR*, Sheffield, South Yorkshire, UK, July, pp. 590–591 (2004).

[80] Christel, M.G., and Moraveji, N., Finding the right shots: assessing usability and performance of a digital video library interface, in *Proc. ACM Multimedia*, New York, pp. 732–739 (2004).

[81] von Ahn, L., and Dabbish, L., Designing games with a purpose, *Commun. ACM*, **51**(8), 58–67 (2008).

[82] Taskiran, C.M., Pizlo, Z., Amir, A., Ponceleon, D., and Delp, E.J., Automated video program summarization using speech transcripts, *IEEE Trans. Multimedia*, **8**(4), 775–791 (2006). 10.1109/TMM.2006.876282

[83] Lee, H., and Smeaton, A.F., Designing the user interface for the Físchlár digital video library, *J. Digital Inf.*, **2**(4), Article No. 103, 2002-05-2, http://jodi.tamu.edu/Articles/v02/i04/Lee/ (2002).

[84] Hughes, A., Wilkens, T., Wildemuth, B., and Marchionini, G., Text or pictures? An eye-tracking study of how people view digital video surrogates. In *Proc. Conf. Image and Video Retrieval (CIVR)* (Urbana-Champaign, IL), 271–280 (2003).

[85] Christel, M.G., and Warmack, A.S., The effect of text in storyboards for video navigation, in *Proc. IEEE International Conference on Acoustics, Speech, and Signal Processing (ICASSP)*, Salt Lake City, UT, May, Vol. III, pp. 1409–1412 (2001). 10.1109/ICASSP.2001.941193

[86] Wildemuth, B.M., Marchionini, G., Wilkens, T., Yang, M., Geisler, G., Fowler, B., Hughes, A., and Mu, X., Alternative surrogates for video objects in a digital library: users' perspectives on their relative usability, in *Proc. 6th European Conf. on Research and Advanced Technology for Digital Libraries* (Sept.) LNCS 2458 (M. Agosti and C. Thanos, Eds.), Springer-Verlag, London, pp. 493–507 (2002).

[87] Song, Y., and Marchionini, G., Effects of audio and visual surrogates for making sense of digital video, in *Proc. ACM CHI '07*, San Jose, CA, April–May, pp. 867–876 (2007). http://doi.acm.org/10.1145/1240624.1240755

[88] ACM, *Proc. ACM Int'l Workshop on TRECVID Video Summarization* (Augsburg, Germany, in conjunction with ACM Multimedia, Sept. 28, 2007), ISBN: 978-1-59593-780-3 (2007).

[89] Mills, M., Cohen, J., and Wong, Y.Y., A magnifier tool for video data. In *Proc. SIGCHI Conference on Human Factors in Computing Systems*, Monterey, CA, May, pp. 93–98 (1992).

[90] Wildemuth, B.M., Marchionini, G., Yang, M., Geisler, G., Wilkens, T., Hughes, A., and Gruss, R., How fast is too fast? Evaluating fast forward surrogates for digital video, in *Proc. Joint Conf. Digital Libraries*, Houston, TX, May, pp. 221–230 (2003).

[91] Christel, M., Lin, W.-H., and Maher, B., Evaluating audio skimming and frame rate acceleration for summarizing BBC Rushes, in *Proc. International Conference on Image and Video Retrieval (CIVR)*, Niagara Falls, Canada, July, pp. 407–416 (2008). http://doi.acm.org/10.1145/1386352.1386405

[92] Christel, M., Hauptmann, A., Lin, W.-H., Chen, M.-Y., Yang, J., Maher, B., and Baron, R., Exploring the utility of fast-forward surrogates for BBC rushes, in *Proc. TRECVID Summarization Workshop* (in assoc. with ACM Multimedia 2008), Vancouver, Canada, October (2008).

[93]   Christel, M., Supporting video library exploratory search: when storyboards are not enough, in *Proc. International Conference on Image and Video Retrieval (CIVR)*, Niagara Falls, Canada, July, pp. 447–456 (2008). http://doi.acm.org/10.1145/1386352.1386410

[94]   Christel, M., Windowing time in digital libraries, in *Proc. ACM/IEEE-CS Joint Conference on Digital Libraries*, Chapel Hill, NC, June, pp. 190–191 (2006). 10.1145/1141753.1141793

[95]   Olsen, K.A., Korfhage, R.R., Sochats, K.M., Spring, M.B., and Williams, J.G., Visualization of a document collection: the VIBE system, *Inf. Process. Manage.*, **29**(1), 69–81 (1993).

[96]   Christel, M.G., Hauptmann, A.G., Wactlar, H.D., and Ng, T.D., Collages as dynamic summaries for news video, in *Proc. ACM Multimedia*, Juan-les-Pins, France, pp. 561–569 (2002).

[97]   Frøkjær, E., Hertzum, M., and Hornbæk, K., Measuring usability: are effectiveness, efficiency, and satisfaction really correlated?, in *Proc. ACM CHI '00*, The Hague Netherlands, April, pp. 345–352 (2000).

[98]   Foraker Design, Usability in Website and Software Design (2008), http://www.usabilityfirst.com/, accessed Oct. 2008.

[99]   Christel, M.G., and Martin, D., Information visualization within a digital video library, *J. Intell. Inf. Syst.*, **11**, 235–257 (1998). 10.1023/A:1008638024786

[100] Christel, M.G., Accessing news libraries through dynamic information extraction, summarization, and visualization, in *Visual Interfaces to Digital Libraries LNCS 2539* (K. Börner and C. Chen, eds.), Springer-Verlag, Berlin (2002).

[101] Nielsen, J., and Molich, R., Heuristic evaluation of user interfaces, in *Proc. ACM CHI*, Seattle, WA, April, pp. 249–256 (1990). http://doi.acm.org/10.1145/97243.97281

[102] Nielsen, J., Heuristic evaluation, in *Usability Inspection Methods* (J. Nielsen, and R.L. Mack, eds.), John Wiley and Sons, New York, NY (1994).

[103] Nielsen, J., Clemmensen, T., and Yssing, C.,. Getting access to what goes on in people's heads? reflections on the think-aloud technique, in *Proc. ACM Nordic CHI*, Aarhus, Denmark, October, pp. 101–110 (2002). http://doi.acm.org/10.1145/572020.572033

[104] Christel, M.G., and Conescu, R., Addressing the challenge of visual information access from digital image and video libraries, in *Proc. Joint Conference on Digital Libraries*, Denver, May, pp. 69–78 (2005). http://doi.acm.org/10.1145/1065385.1065402

[105] Christel, M.G., and Conescu, R., Mining novice user activity with TRECVID interactive retrieval tasks, in *Proc. Conf. Image and Video Retrieval (LNCS 4071)*, pp. 21–30 (2006). 10.1007/11788034_3

[106] Enser, P.G.B., and Sandom, C.J., retrieval of archival moving imagery—CBIR outside the frame?, in *Image and Video Retrieval (CIVR 2002 Proceedings)*, pp. 206–214 (2002).

[107] Girgensohn, A., Adcock, J., Cooper, M., and Wilcox, L., Interactive search in large video collections, in *CHI '05 Extended Abstracts on Human Factors in Computing Systems*, ACM Press, NY, pp. 1395–1398 (2005).

[93]   Christel, M., Supporting video library exploratory search: when storyboards are not enough, in *Proc. International Conference on Image and Video Retrieval (CIVR)*, Niagara Falls, Canada, July, pp. 447–456 (2008). http://doi.acm.org/10.1145/1386352.1386410

[94]   Christel, M., Windowing time in digital libraries, in *Proc. ACM/IEEE-CS Joint Conference on Digital Libraries*, Chapel Hill, NC, June, pp. 190–191 (2006). 10.1145/1141753.1141793

[95]   Olsen, K.A., Korfhage, R.R., Sochats, K.M., Spring, M.B., and Williams, J.G., Visualization of a document collection: the VIBE system, *Inf. Process. Manage.*, **29**(1), 69–81 (1993).

[96]   Christel, M.G., Hauptmann, A.G., Wactlar, H.D., and Ng, T.D., Collages as dynamic summaries for news video, in *Proc. ACM Multimedia*, Juan-les-Pins, France, pp. 561–569 (2002).

[97]   Frøkjær, E., Hertzum, M., and Hornbæk, K., Measuring usability: are effectiveness, efficiency, and satisfaction really correlated?, in *Proc. ACM CHI '00*, The Hague Netherlands, April, pp. 345–352 (2000).

[98]   Foraker Design, Usability in Website and Software Design (2008), http://www.usabilityfirst.com/, accessed Oct. 2008.

[99]   Christel, M.G., and Martin, D., Information visualization within a digital video library, *J. Intell. Inf. Syst.*, **11**, 235–257 (1998). 10.1023/A:1008638024786

[100] Christel, M.G., Accessing news libraries through dynamic information extraction, summarization, and visualization, in *Visual Interfaces to Digital Libraries LNCS 2539* (K. Börner and C. Chen, eds.), Springer-Verlag, Berlin (2002).

[101] Nielsen, J., and Molich, R., Heuristic evaluation of user interfaces, in *Proc. ACM CHI*, Seattle, WA, April, pp. 249–256 (1990). http://doi.acm.org/10.1145/97243.97281

[102] Nielsen, J., Heuristic evaluation, in *Usability Inspection Methods* (J. Nielsen, and R.L. Mack, eds.), John Wiley and Sons, New York, NY (1994).

[103] Nielsen, J., Clemmensen, T., and Yssing, C.,. Getting access to what goes on in people's heads? reflections on the think-aloud technique, in *Proc. ACM Nordic CHI*, Aarhus, Denmark, October, pp. 101–110 (2002). http://doi.acm.org/10.1145/572020.572033

[104] Christel, M.G., and Conescu, R., Addressing the challenge of visual information access from digital image and video libraries, in *Proc. Joint Conference on Digital Libraries*, Denver, May, pp. 69–78 (2005). http://doi.acm.org/10.1145/1065385.1065402

[105] Christel, M.G., and Conescu, R., Mining novice user activity with TRECVID interactive retrieval tasks, in *Proc. Conf. Image and Video Retrieval (LNCS 4071)*, pp. 21–30 (2006). 10.1007/11788034_3

[106] Enser, P.G.B., and Sandom, C.J., retrieval of archival moving imagery—CBIR outside the frame?, in *Image and Video Retrieval (CIVR 2002 Proceedings)*, pp. 206–214 (2002).

[107] Girgensohn, A., Adcock, J., Cooper, M., and Wilcox, L., Interactive search in large video collections, in *CHI '05 Extended Abstracts on Human Factors in Computing Systems*, ACM Press, NY, pp. 1395–1398 (2005).

[82] Taskiran, C.M., Pizlo, Z., Amir, A., Ponceleon, D., and Delp, E.J., Automated video program summarization using speech transcripts, *IEEE Trans. Multimedia*, **8**(4), 775–791 (2006). 10.1109/TMM.2006.876282

[83] Lee, H., and Smeaton, A.F., Designing the user interface for the Físchlár digital video library, *J. Digital Inf.*, **2**(4), Article No. 103, 2002-05-2, http://jodi.tamu.edu/Articles/v02/ i04/Lee/ (2002).

[84] Hughes, A., Wilkens, T., Wildemuth, B., and Marchionini, G., Text or pictures? An eye-tracking study of how people view digital video surrogates. In *Proc. Conf. Image and Video Retrieval (CIVR)* (Urbana-Champaign, IL), 271–280 (2003).

[85] Christel, M.G., and Warmack, A.S., The effect of text in storyboards for video navigation, in *Proc. IEEE International Conference on Acoustics, Speech, and Signal Processing (ICASSP)*, Salt Lake City, UT, May, Vol. III, pp. 1409–1412 (2001). 10.1109/ICASSP.2001.941193

[86] Wildemuth, B.M., Marchionini, G., Wilkens, T., Yang, M., Geisler, G., Fowler, B., Hughes, A., and Mu, X., Alternative surrogates for video objects in a digital library: users' perspectives on their relative usability, in *Proc. 6th European Conf. on Research and Advanced Technology for Digital Libraries* (Sept.) LNCS 2458 (M. Agosti and C. Thanos, Eds.), Springer-Verlag, London, pp. 493–507 (2002).

[87] Song, Y., and Marchionini, G., Effects of audio and visual surrogates for making sense of digital video, in *Proc. ACM CHI '07*, San Jose, CA, April–May, pp. 867–876 (2007). http:// doi.acm.org/10.1145/1240624.1240755

[88] ACM, *Proc. ACM Int'l Workshop on TRECVID Video Summarization* (Augsburg, Germany, in conjunction with ACM Multimedia, Sept. 28, 2007), ISBN: 978-1-59593-780-3 (2007).

[89] Mills, M., Cohen, J., and Wong, Y.Y., A magnifier tool for video data. In *Proc. SIGCHI Conference on Human Factors in Computing Systems*, Monterey, CA, May, pp. 93–98 (1992).

[90] Wildemuth, B.M., Marchionini, G., Yang, M., Geisler, G., Wilkens, T., Hughes, A., and Gruss, R., How fast is too fast? Evaluating fast forward surrogates for digital video, in *Proc. Joint Conf. Digital Libraries*, Houston, TX, May, pp. 221–230 (2003).

[91] Christel, M., Lin, W.-H., and Maher, B., Evaluating audio skimming and frame rate acceleration for summarizing BBC Rushes, in *Proc. International Conference on Image and Video Retrieval (CIVR)*, Niagara Falls, Canada, July, pp. 407–416 (2008). http://doi.acm. org/10.1145/1386352.1386405

[92] Christel, M., Hauptmann, A., Lin, W.-H., Chen, M.-Y., Yang, J., Maher, B., and Baron, R., Exploring the utility of fast-forward surrogates for BBC rushes, in *Proc. TRECVID Summarization Workshop* (in assoc. with ACM Multimedia 2008), Vancouver, Canada, October (2008).

[108] Hollink, L., Nguyen, G.P., Koelma, D.C., Schreiber, A.T., and Worring, M., Assessing user behaviour in news video retrieval, *IEEE Proc. Vision, Image, Signal Process.*, **152**(6), 911–918 (2005). 10.1049/ip-vis:20045187

[109] Christel, M.G., Establishing the utility of non-text search for news video retrieval with real world users, in *Proc. ACM Multimedia*, Augsburg, Germany, September, pp. 706–717 (2007). http://doi.acm.org/10.1145/1291233.1291395

[110] Shneiderman, B., Byrd, D., and Croft, W.B., Clarifying search: a user-interface framework for text searches, *D-Lib Mag.*, **3**, 1 (January), http://www.dlib.org.

[111] White, R.W., Kules, B., Drucker, S.M., schraefel, M.C., Supporting exploratory search, introduction, *Commun. ACM*, **49**(4), 36–39 (2006).

[112] Marchionini, G., Exploratory search: from finding to understanding, *Commun. ACM*, **49**(4), 41–46 (2006). http://doi.acm.org/10.1145/1121949.1121979

[113] Christel, M., and Frisch, M., Evaluating the contributions of video representation for a life oral history collection, in *Proc. ACM/IEEE-CS Joint Conference on Digital Libraries*, Pittsburgh, PA, June, pp. 241–250 (2008). http://doi.acm.org/10.1145/1378889.1378929

[114] Shneiderman, B., and Plaisant, C., Strategies for evaluating information visualization tools: multidimensional in-depth long-term case studies, in *Proc. Beyond Time and Errors: Novel Evaluation Methods for Information Visualization, Workshop of the Advanced Visual Interfaces Conference*, pp. 1–7 (2006). http://doi.acm.org/10.1145/1168149.1168158

[115] Gersh, J., Lewis, B., et al., Supporting insight-based information exploration in intelligence analysis, *Commun. ACM*, **49**(4), 63–68 (2006).

[116] Marchionini, G., and Geisler, G., The open video digital library, *D-Lib Mag.*, **8**(12) (2002), www.dlib.org.

[117] Thomas, J.J., and Cook, K.A., A visual analytics agenda, *IEEE Comput. Graph. Appl.*, **26**(1), 10–13 (2006).

[118] Thomas, J.J., and Cook, K.A., Eds., *Illuminating the Path—Research and Development Agenda for Visual Analytics*, IEEE Press, Los Alamitos, CA (2004–2008). Downloadable at http://nvac.pnl.gov/agenda.stm.

[119] Hauptmann, A.G., Lin, W.-H., Yan, R., Yang, J., and Chen, M.-Y., Extreme video retrieval: joint maximization of human and computer performance, in *Proc. ACM Multimedia*, Santa Barbara, CA, October, pp. 385–394 (2006). http://doi.acm.org/10.1145/1180639.1180721

[120] Shneiderman, B., The eyes have it: a task by data type taxonomy for information visualizations, in *Proc. IEEE Symposium on Visual Languages*, Boulder, CO, Sept., pp. 336–343 (1996).

[121] Google, GAUDI: Google Audio Indexing (2008), http://labs.google.com/gaudi, accessed Oct. 2008.

Author Biography

Michael G. Christel has worked at Carnegie Mellon University (CMU), Pittsburgh, PA, since 1987, first with the Software Engineering Institute, and since 1997 as a senior systems scientist in the School of Computer Science. In September 2008, he accepted a position as research professor in CMU's Entertainment Technology Center (ETC). He is a founding member of the Informedia research team at CMU designing, deploying, and evaluating video analysis and retrieval systems for use in education, health care, humanities research, and situation analysis. His research interests focus on the convergence of multimedia processing, information visualization, and digital library research. He has published more than 50 conference and journal papers in related areas, serves on the Program Committee for various multimedia and digital library IEEE-CS and ACM conferences, and is an associate editor for *IEEE Transactions on Multimedia*. He has worked with digital video since its inception in 1987, and received his PhD from the Georgia Institute of Technology, Atlanta, GA, in 1991, with his thesis examining digital video interfaces for software engineering training. He received his bachelor's degree in mathematics and computer science from Canisius College, Buffalo, NY, in 1983. At the ETC, Christel hopes to broaden his research focus from multimedia for information search and retrieval, to multimedia for information engagement and edutainment, with users being both producers and consumers of multimedia content.

Printed in the United States
by Baker & Taylor Publisher Services